THE SHAMAN'S TRANSFORMATION
BOOK 2 OF THE SHAMANIC MYSTERIES

Norman W. Wilson PhD

THE SHAMAN'S TRANSFORMATION
BOOK 2 OF THE SHAMANIC MYSTERIES

A ZADKIEL PUBLISHING PAPERBACK

© Copyright 2018
Norman W. Wilson PhD

The right of Norman W. Wilson to be identified as author and channel of this work has been asserted by him in accordance with the Copyright, Designs and Patents Act 1988.

All Rights Reserved

No reproduction, copy or transmission of the publication may be made without written permission.

No paragraph of this publication may be reproduced, copied or transmitted save with the written permission of the publisher, or in accordance with the provisions of the Copyright Act 1956 (as amended).

Any person who does any unauthorised act in relation to this publication may be liable to criminal prosecution and civil claims for damages.

ISBN: 978-1-78695-197-7

Zadkiel Publishing
An Imprint of Fiction4All
www.fiction4all.com

This Edition
Published 2018

FOR

SUZANNE VOTRAW WILSON

O' Great Spirits

Whose voices the winds carry
Whose Being gives life to the Universe,
   Hear me.

I am Adam, Man of the Earth,
Grant me your guidance and wisdom
   Show me how to walk in beauty.

Fill my being with wonder and joy
Fill my heart with love and respect for
   All things created by you.

I am Adam, Man of the Universe,
Reveal all that you would have me know,
   Help me love that which I don't.

Give me patience where I have none,
I am Adam, Man of Man
   Teach me Your song of life.

APPRECIATION

I am deeply grateful to my late friend and mentor, Charlotte- Boyett Compo for her line by line edit, for her encouragement.

Jacquie Rogers is owed a great debt of gratitude for the hours spent in teaching me formatting, editing, and a whole bag full of neat time saving tricks in word processing.

To Suzanne for her gracious and loving support.

To Stuart Holland for his guidance in bringing this version to life.

ALSO BY NORMAN W. WILSON

Shamanism: What It's All About
The Shaman's Quest
How to Get What You REALLY Want
The Making of A Shaman
Healing-The Shaman's Way
Activating Your Spirit Guides-The Shaman's Way

CHAPTER 1 - THE FUNERAL

**Kill reverence and you've killed the hero in man.
Ayn Rand**

There had been an end to an earthly life. A couple of nights before his death I remember waking up. He was calling my name. I can still hear his voice saying, "Seek and you shall find." He always said that when he didn't have an answer to my questions. I should have known then, he was cashing it in. They told me he sat up on the edge of the bed and simply said, "Now!" and died. His soul-self is finally free to go its own way.

One of his Veteran friends from the town picked me up at the airport. From there it was about an hour and a half drive to the small town in which he had spent his entire life and in which his burial is to take place. And, I'm sure, soon to be forgotten. His friend dropped me at my hotel, an old brick building, built back in the mid-1800's. Plastered over and painted a bright yellow, it stands as a beacon for all to see. I had just time enough to change from the jeans into a suit and tie appropriate for a wake.

At the funeral home, I thought it odd there weren't more people present, especially since he had always lived here. I paid my respects to the two women seated by the casket.

The old one said, "Thank you for coming."

The younger woman nodded. Said nothing.

I took a seat in the last row of chairs set up for the mourners. There might have been twenty people present. I thought someone might step forward to speak, to talk about his life, to tell those present, he was a hero, that he had served his country well, and he had been awarded the Purple Heart. No one did.

At the church service the next morning, a few more people showed up. The church, a massive stone structure, was a miniature cathedral. Large hand carved beams arched the ceiling with their interior spaces broken up with long hanging lighted orbs. The pews were of dark wood and cushioned with plush green velvet. The sanctuary's wall was of white marble with an inlaid gold leaf of The Christ figure. Stained glass windows telling the story of The Christ lined both sides of the nave creating kaleidoscopic patterns throughout the church. His casket draped with an American flag sat in front of a raised polished marble altar. On it was a single gold cross covered with a black veil.

As I looked around, I noticed a few mourners with the appropriate tears and the dabbing of eyes with a tissue. You know the type–doing whatever they think social custom demands and nothing more. Each relieved they were not the one in the casket. I'm sure if this funeral had taken place in certain other countries there would have been much pulling of hair, gnashing of teeth and moaning, an outward pouring of grief and respect for the deceased. At graveside, only the old woman in her wheelchair cried out as she threw a handful of dirt upon his coffin. I suppose they wondered why there were no tears in my eyes.

One of the mourners came up to me and said, "Why did you come?"

He got no reply from me. I simply stared through him. What a pompous ass I thought to myself. He and his father owned one of the local stores. Unlike the man in the grave, they were not of this town. I was.

"Why did you come?" he asked again, taking hold of my arm.

With a slight pressure on his arm as I removed his hand and with a nudge of my foot he landed on his backside. Leaning toward him and in a tone as cold as the weather, I replied, "To pay my respects. Isn't that why you are here?"

With that I walked away leaving him in a puddle of mud created by the hearse. Old resentments welled up and flooded me with bitter memories of his arrogance, memories I didn't want.

Years ago, we had had an argument and he had paid two guys twenty bucks to beat me up. Even though I came out of it with only a black eye, I still resented the fact he didn't have the guts to fight me himself. We must have been about twelve or thirteen years old.

As I slid into the backseat of the car that had brought me to the cemetery, I felt sudden twinge in my rib cage. That quickly refocused my attention. After the gravesite service, there was the traditional reception at the deceased's home. Those present toasted his memory with a glass of red wine. I didn't raise my glass; there was nothing in it. I felt that's how they viewed his life, empty and nothing in it, and I wasn't buying into that. He was so much more but they— they, never took the time to find out.

The town itself was like that—empty! At one time, it may have been different, maybe back in the 1880's. Yet, it's still a pretty town, surrounded by seven hills but now like so many other things here, they too are barren. The locals always liked to say, "Just like Rome" when anyone mentioned the hills. In addition to the tourist, a granary was the only other major industry. It employed only thirty people at peak times. The rest of those who worked did so in a neighboring state. The houses were large wooden structures, some three stories high. Many had curved porches while others had the typical columns favored by Thomas Jefferson. Of course, not everyone lived in these grand houses. Once you left three of the main entrances into the town, there were smaller homes, and like any small town, it had its share of run-down old derelicts. The fourth entrance into town offered the visitor a bar of questionable reputation, a sewer treatment plant, a junkyard, a used car dealership, and the town's electrical power plant. The entrance you used influenced your attitude about the town.

Back in my hotel room, and looking out its solitary window, I watched cars going up and down Main Street. It was a narrow brick street with a wide meridian separating the two lanes. During spring and summer, the meridian had an ample supply of flowers and well-manicured grass. Winter made it barren. Down its center, lined up soldier-like and standing at attention were gas streetlights, cold, sterile, and unmoved by the continual parade of cars. At some point, I realized the same cars were going up and down the street made even narrower by other diagonally parked cars. With a herd mentality, they followed each other. It occurred to me, they represented the sum and total of the aspirations of the people behind the wheels. The hotel window began to steam up and the view outside took on a yellow surrealistic montage, a massive nondescript blur of shifting steel, glass, and plastic punctuated with splashes of red as someone applied his brakes. Putting on my topcoat, the one I bought for the funeral, I went down to the street.

The cold crisp air felt good in spite of the fumes from the parked cars whose motors idled to keep those inside warm. As I walked west, I noticed a few people in the darkened cars light their cigarettes and sometimes there would be the small red glow as someone took a drag.

Ah 'Saturday Night Live' in small town USA, I thought.

A door flung open and a middle aged man staggered out onto the street. Loud western music followed him until the door's closing silenced its sound. Horns honked, the 4X4's gunned their motors, and the bass blaring from their radios vibrated an unnatural rhythm. These were the high school jocks enjoying their shift at cruising Main Street. The next group, the 20 to 30 year-olds, would be out in their bigger trucks, SUVs, and Jeeps, radios blaring honky-tonk, announcing their serious intent to stud.

The little park at the center of town with its Civil War statues and narrow sidewalks emanating from a large fountain offered a quiet refuge from the traffic. The gaslights flooding the area with their pale yellow light helped to smother the intrusive traffic sounds. Once I got to the fountain, I sat down on a bench and began to study the figures in its center. There was no bubbling water gushing over the figures. Never is at this time of year. Too cold. The park bench reminded me of that, yet I continued to sit trying to remember a long forgotten past. How many hours had I spent sitting here with him, listening to his earthy wisdom? When had I first met him?

It really wasn't all that long ago or was it? For a time I thought he was the one who was going to answer my myriad questions. It took me awhile to accept the fact I was mistaken. I felt he didn't want to share the secrets of life with me. As time separated us, I realized he could only tell me what he knew and his struggle to find examples to illustrate his points turned out to be simply an effort to illustrate the same points over and over again. I don't fault him. If there is any fault it is mine for asking questions, he could not answer. All of this transpired before I found Esaugetuh [1] or should I say before he let me find him. Anyway, here I am freezing my ass off on a park bench in a small town in the middle of winter and still seeking answers. The hissing of snowflakes as they hit the gaslight above me brought me back from my short trip down memory's lane. Getting up from the cold bench, I headed back to my hotel.

Once there, the night clerk told me someone was waiting for me in the hotel's bar. The bar was a long narrow room, dimly lit, smelly from stale cigarette smoke. Empty beer bottles sat on unoccupied tables. As I walked in, its wooden floor creaked its own welcome. It took a few minutes for my eyes to adjust to the poor lighting. A single solitary figure sat at the bar, no one I recognized, and the only occupant other than the bartender. All I could detect was a mop of long dark hair.

"Buy you a drink, Adam?"

"Running-water?"

"The very same. You sure have been hard to find." he replied. "Where have you been? I've been trying to find you for over a year."

"Around. What do you want with me?"

"For one thing I want to know about Esaugetuh. Where is he? What happened after you left the West Coast? I lost track of you north of Seattle."

"Off the record?" I said, remembering he was a newspaper reporter.

"Okay, off the record." Running-water replied, tipping his glass in salute.

"By the way, why Running-water?" I asked. "Do you have another name?"

"My mother said it was an appropriate name because as a baby I always had wet pants," he laughed. "And I still do and it's not because I can't hold my water." he continued, still laughing. "It's Paul Dakota. After Saint Paul. My mother covered both bases that way, Native traditions and Christian beliefs."

We sat there with quiet reigning between us. Just a quiet kind of quiet. Each giving the other time and respect.

Wonder what he really wants, I thought.

"Adam, what really happened after you and Esaugetuh left Seattle? Where did the two of you go and where is he now?" Running-water said, breaking the silence between us.

"I'm not sure I can or even want to tell you or anyone else for that matter. It's still so intense." I replied.

"Share that with me and I'll tell you something I bet you don't know," Running-water said as he shoved his long black hair back from his face. It was a handsome face, finely chiseled, with high cheek bones in keeping with his origins.

"I know you and your little secrets. You're always trying to bait me with some morsel of information about Esaugetuh. So, what is it this time? Spit it out."

"I know where he lives." Running-water said as his dark eyes sparkled, revealing his inner delight.

"Big deal! He lives in Canada. Nothing new about that."

"I mean his house." Running-water said.

"You're putting me on."

"No! After we left Mesa Verde, you headed for Seattle and I eventually went home to Albuquerque. There was a letter from Esaugetuh."

"In this letter he told you where he lived."

"No. The return address told me that. The letter contained another envelope with your name on it. He asked me to find you and give you the other envelope." Running-water said as he handed me an envelope.

"This has been opened."

"I opened it. I shouldn't have, but no harm done, right?"

As I began removing the contents of the envelope Running-water interrupted, "He's turned everything over to you. You are one very rich man. He even gave you his house. So when do we leave?"

I stopped, turning to Running-water I said, "We're not going anywhere. Not now, not later, not ever!"

"But—."

"No buts. You've violated any semblance of a relationship we had by reading a private letter addressed to me, a letter placed in your trust. You broke that trust. No harm done? What a joke! There's no way in hell that I can ever believe you have even an ounce of integrity."

I got up from the barstool, threw a five on the counter. "I pay my own way."

The elevator creaked and groaned as it chugalugged up to the third floor. Back in my room, I decided to leave immediately instead of waiting until tomorrow when my return flight was scheduled. I was sure Running-water would not leave me alone.

After throwing my stuff into my suitcase, I called the desk and asked them to get me a cab if the town had one. Luck was with me. There was a man who did drive people into the city or to the airport. I asked that he pick me up at a side door hoping that Running-water wouldn't see me leaving. It wasn't exactly a cab but the 1960's Buick was just fine.

The road was a narrow two-lane black top with a number of sharp curves. The snow that had begun falling earlier had accumulated and patches of black ice had formed forcing the driver to slow. Fortunately, he wasn't prone to talking and that left me to my own thoughts.

There wasn't much heat in the back seat of the old Buick. In an effort to keep warm I pulled my coat collar up and then dug my hands deeper into my coat pockets. As I did I felt the folded letter from Esaugetuh and somehow its presence made me feel better. The physical cold, the emotional coldness of the town and the lack of any sincere emotions by most of those at the funeral had left me numb. I would wait until another time to read the contents of the letter.

"Guess you haven't learned much."

"Driver, what did you say?" I said, leaning forward.

"Sir?"

"I asked what you just said." I replied tersely.

"Nothing. Can't talk and drive at the same time. The road's slick."

I was sure he had said something but I didn't pursue it any further. Even though considerable time had lapsed, we had traveled only a few miles. The driver pulled the car to the side of the road and stopped.

"Why are we stopping?"

"Need to put chains on. Should a done it before we left."

"Can I help?"

"No. It's best you stay in the car. You city fellas ain't used to this."

I remained in the car. No use aggravating him. There weren't any other vehicles on the road. Even the big eighteen wheelers weren't moving tonight. The old Buick suddenly lurched forward and there was a terrible scream. I jumped out of the car. He was thrashing around on the ground, holding up his bloody hand.

"You got a first aid kit in the car?" I asked.

I looked. There was none.

"Okay, lay still and do exactly as I tell you. Close your eyes."

Kneeling by his side, I cupped his injured hand between both of mine. I felt the stickiness of his warm blood as I applied a gentle pressure to his injuries.

"My hand feels hot. Am I going to lose my hand? He whispered.

"Don't talk. Lay perfectly still and don't move until I say so"

We remained that way for over thirty minutes. The bleeding stopped but unfortunately, the snow had not. I placed his hand on his chest, got up, went to the car, opened my suitcase, and pulled out a clean white shirt, tore it into long strips and wrapped each around his injured hand. With his hand in bandages, he got up, climbed into the back of the car, and laid down. I covered him up with my coat.

Once I had the chains on, I slide behind the wheel. We were in the midst of a whiteout and we couldn't stay where we were.

Putting the car into low gear, I eased it back onto the highway and continued to head north. The headlights were of little use. Their only value being that they showed the reflectors on the guardrails and that told me I was at least partially on the road. Once or twice, I scraped a couple guard rails, and leaving, I am sure, some pretty deep scratches on his car.

Five hours later, we pulled into the entrance of the airport. With the help of an attendant, I got my driver into the terminal. There I removed the bandages, washed the wound, and re-bandaged it. Fortunately, they had a well-equipped first aid kit.

"Man, he sure bled a lot for such a small wound." The attendant said looking at our blood stained clothes.

"Heavy bleeder, quick healer," I replied. "Could you get him a double shot of brandy and put it in hot water?" I asked handing the attendant a twenty. "Keep the change for your trouble."

"No problem," replied the attendant as he disappeared around a corner.

Flight cancellations lit up the board. Depending on the weather, my flight is set for late tomorrow afternoon. In a strange way, I was grateful for the storm because it closed the roads and Running-water wouldn't be able to get out of town and follow me. At least for the time being I was safe from his intrusion.

The brandy arrived and with two gulps, the driver drained the glass. It didn't take long for it to work. While he slept, I opened the letter from Esaugetuh.

It was as Running-water said, Esaugetuh had turned his estate over to me. There was a sizable chunk of land consisting of four sections at 640 acres per section. In addition to savings and checking accounts, certificates of deposit, dozens of shares of stocks in major world corporations, there were several vehicles, office-apartment buildings, his place of residence, and a Gulfstream Jet.

That explains how he got around, I thought.

There was a safety deposit box at a Montreal bank. I looked for the key but it wasn't there. A quick search of my coat pockets produced nothing. I hurried out to the car, but a search turned up nothing. Back into the terminal, it hit me. Running-water's protest at my not letting him join me was not forceful enough. I should have known he was up to something. He kept the key to insure he would be going with me.

"Damn him," I said out loud.

At that, the driver woke up. "What? What is it?"

"It's okay. You've been sleeping. Let's take a look at that hand," I replied.

He unwrapped his bandaged hand, held it up toward the lights, opened and closed the fingers, and then slowly spread them apart. He was sucking so much air I was sure he was going to pass out.

With a near hysterical laugh he said, "There's nothing wrong with my hand. My fingers are okay. How can that be? I know I smashed the hell out of them fingers."

"You must have thought you smashed them worse than you did. The slight swelling will go away."

"No! I know there was blood all over the place. My fingers were minced meat. What did you do to me? I remember feeling intense heat on my hand, real hot. Who are you?"

"Just your passenger. I bandaged your hand and that's all there is to it. I need to go back. I left something at the hotel."

"It'll cost you another fifty. No, make that a hundred. I have to have something for my time."

"I'll double that if you forget what happened. Also, I'll pay for the repair to your car."

"What's wrong with my car?"

"A few scratches. Nothing that can't be fixed," I replied. "Now can we get going?"

The snow had stopped and the wind died down. The plows and sanders had been out and had done a good job. The roads were passable. The driver kept looking at his hand and then would shake his head.

"Nobody would believe me anyway. Nobody," he repeated over and over.

Once back in town I paid the driver and at the same time hired him to take me back to the airport. In the hotel lobby, Running-water was waiting for me.

"Thought you'd be back," he said with a sheepish grin.

"Hand it over and do it now!" I said as I slammed him against the wall.

I pulled my clinched fist back to rearrange his perfect teeth. I heard it again. The same voice I heard in the car.

"You haven't learned much, have you?"

Shame rushed over me and I let go of Running-water and dropped my fist. Esaugetuh's words popped into my head, 'Accept everything as having value.'

"Shit man! I thought we were friends. Here's your damn key," he said shaken by the force of my anger.

I took the key and started to leave. Something turned me around and I caught tears in his eyes. He turned his head to look away from me.

Again, I felt the rush of shame.

"Look," I said, "I don't know if Esaugetuh is alive or dead. Any thought of going into his house, of going through his things just blew me away. I'm sorry that I lost my cool."

Once more, I felt a twinge in my rib cage. Shrugging it off, I extended my hand to Running-water, "Can we start over again?"

"Sure. Can you?" he replied as he shook my hand.

CHAPTER 2 - AND SO IT BEGINS ALL OVER AGAIN

What gives life its value you can find—and lose. But never possess. This holds good above all for the Truth about Life.
Dag Hammarskjöld

"You going to Montreal to open the box?" Runningwater asked.

"No. Esaugetuh never had me sign a signature card for any bank. You have to sign in when you want to open a safety deposit box."

"But he must have known that and since he did why'd he leave you the key if your name wasn't at the bank?

"Good point," I replied, "but I don't see how he got my signature on the authorization card. I don't think he would have forged it. "

"Didn't you register at the Mesa Verde conference?"

"Of course, everyone who attended had to sign in," I replied.

"And how did you sign in?"

"I filled out a card with my name, address, and signed it just like everyone else."

"Wrong! You signed an authorization card for the bank. Those, like you, who arrived on the whisper of the wind simply signed a tablet and were given whatever camp slot was available."

"Hmm! I also registered at his motel in Florida and it was a card there also. Okay, so my signature may or may not be at the Montreal bank. I'm not going there right now. I was on my way elsewhere when I got notice of the funeral. I need to continue with that trip." I said.

"Okay. When do we leave? Running-water asked.

"We don't," I said remembering my last outburst at his question. "Why don't you head on into Canada and see what you can find out there? Then we can meet up sometime down the line."

"You sure it wouldn't be better if we went together?"

"Yes. You are a Native and most likely, you'll get better information than I would. Also, don't mention my name. It may cause suspicion among the people you talk to."

With that settled, I met my driver and we once again headed for the airport. I was on my way to Lake Tahoe when I got the message about my old friend's death. I had wanted to go back to the Cathedral of Trees where the rangers found me. Perhaps there I could get some sense of what really occurred. Furthermore, there might be some clues as to what became of Esaugetuh. My heart rate kicked up several notches just thinking about it. My breathing quickened to the point of near hyperventilation. There are so many mixed feelings, horrors terrifyingly real, and beautiful beyond compare. Beads of sweat trickled down my face and I felt my body wracked with uncontrolled spasms of shaking. It was strange observing my body doing whatever it wanted to and the *I-of-me* could do nothing about it. For the remainder of the trip to the airport, I laid in the fetal position on the back seat of the car with my topcoat pulled tight around me.

At the airport, the driver received his money and an extra hundred for his time. As I checked in at the counter, he came back and handed me all of the money.

"Can't take it. Not after this. "He said holding up his healed hand. " Don't know what you did, mister, but I'm grateful to have my hand. Anytime you are back in this area, the rides are on me."

That said, he turned and left.

My flight schedule is really off the wall. From here, I fly to Buffalo, from there to Atlanta, then to Denver, and from there to Reno. At Reno, I would use a rental to drive to Lake Tahoe. The Cherokee I wanted wasn't available so there would be a layover in Reno for a couple of days. That was okay with me. I could use a little rest.

After checking in, I decided to walk the streets since the gaming tables were of no interest to me. The glitz of Las Vegas is not present here but some of the people are just as interesting. There were, of course, the tourists in town for a weekend of gambling, the regulars, those who had lost it all, the hangers-on, and the tawdry types. The hawkers at the entrances of the casinos offered a variety of tickets, vouchers, and tour information. There were also those who offered other kinds of services. My mood, instead of improving, grew gloomier. It was impossible for me to come up with a rational explanation of the whole business with the driver's hand; nor do I have an explanation of why I did what I did or how his hand healed within a matter of a few hours.

It's been a long time since the Tahoe incident. Instead of having answers to my ever plaguing questions, I now have more questions coupled with the mysterious disappearance of Esaugetuh.

Sometimes I wake up in the night with cold sweats and yet my hands, having a glow about them, would be warm. The first time I noticed this I tried washing it away. The more I scrubbed the brighter the glow became and my hands grew so hot they were painful.

Another interesting thing I began to notice was that I always placed my right hand over my left when I washed them. With the driver, I had cupped his hand in my left and then placed my right hand on top.

Numerous flashbacks to the forested cathedral in the Lake Tahoe area were a recurring theme in my dreams. Sometimes they were so very real I would wake myself up screaming. On more than one occasion, I had frightened people in the adjoining rooms at the hotels or motels where I was staying. They would call security and then I would have to go through the embarrassment of a room search while those who had made the call would try to peer into my room. Finally, satisfied that no murder had taken place they would shake their heads and return to their rooms. The only thing murdered was my sleep.

It was still relatively early by Reno time when I returned to my hotel room. The long walk about the streets did not ease the tension. The hotel had a resident massage therapist and I decided to take advantage of that service. Perhaps a good rub down would do the trick. Sleep did come but the ringing of the phone ended that. It was the rental agency calling to tell me that they had the Cherokee serviced and ready for me to pick up. I asked them to deliver it.

The drive to Lake Tahoe was an easy one. I stopped to buy enough supplies to last for three days. In addition to food and water, I picked up a couple of lanterns, a shotgun and a box of shells, a pop-up tent, and a backpack. Next, I went to a surveillance store and picked up some items that I would need in my search for clues about Esaugetuh.

Hiking through snow is never easy, the trek into the sacred area of the Cathedral of Trees taxed my energy, and it was necessary to make frequent rest stops. I had not made any preparations for my visit to the sacred grounds, no fasting, no cleansing, nor prayers. I felt there was no need to do so because I had met my demon and survived. I was a part of the place.

Once there I planned to set up camp and do a systematic search of the areas. I would have to be as careful as a forensic expert. Perhaps it would have been better to hire one but then there would be questions that I was not ready to answer.

As I entered the circle of stately trees, they seemed to bow their heads in recognition. Somehow, their whispering comforted me. I thought I would have a difficult time locating the exact spot where Esaugetuh had laid out the seven sacred stones but much to my surprise they were just as he had placed them. There was no snow on them and as I knelt down to touch one a voice boomed, "Why have you come back?"

I spun around but no one was there. Unlike that last time, someone asked me that I was the one flat on his back. They were pushing me into the ground. I cried out in pain. Anger took its grip and then absolute rage. Somewhere from deep within my soul came a tremendous primordial scream.

"I am that I am! Adam awake!"

The earth beneath me shook– a spasm violent enough that the giant trees groaned and bowed their heads as in prayer. [2] A high pitched scream filled the air and the Spirits released their hold on me. Just for an instant, I thought I saw their light streaks, little flashes set off in the night sky.

I continued to lay on the ground too exhausted to set up camp. Sometime later, the smell of smoke brought me to my feet. A small fire blazed in the center of the circle of seven stones. Again I looked around; there were no other footprints, just my own. I checked the spot where I had been laying and it contained a definite indentation and not just in the snow.

In spite of the physical strain just experienced, I made short work of setting up camp. Hot coffee, a can of beans and a biscuit appeased the stomach. Night was descending all too quickly. An owl hooted in a nearby tree and then I heard its wings as it took flight to begin its nightly prowl for prey. Morning would be a better time to begin my search of the area. As I sat by the small fire, I began to pray.

O, Great Spirits
Whose voices the winds carry,
Whose Beings give life to the universe hear me.
I am Adam, man of the Earth
Grant me your guidance and wisdom
Show me how to walk in your beauty; fill my being with wonder and joy.
Fill my heart with love and respect for all things you have created.
I am Adam, man of the Universe.
Let me understand all that you would have me know.
Help me love that which I do not.
Give me patience where I have none
I am Adam, man of Man.
Let me know your song of life.

A rush of wind nearly caused the fire to go out and yet like life itself, it clung to its own being. A chill came over me and I pulled up my coat collar. After securing the fire, I went to bed in the pop-up tent. Strange as it may seem I felt safe and comfortable and didn't feel the need to load the shotgun. A new melody played in my heart and I slept soundly.

The call of a bird announcing the dawn woke me. I felt totally refreshed, something I had not felt in a long, long time. A new strength seemed to surge through my being and I felt good. The sunrise in all its splendor promised a beautiful day. As I looked around, I noticed a set of prints, those of a cougar. Then I noticed where it had sat and finally had lain. As I squatted by its still warm bed, I could smell its presence. Slowly I turned and just in time to catch a glimpse of the very large cat bounding due north. I made a mental note to check that area at a later time.

The task would not be an easy one with the snow and the lapse of time. Any sweeping would take considerable care. In keeping with the significance of the number seven, [3] I began seven feet from the center of the circle of stones and I would work my way around the center, seven feet at a time. I would divide each section into subsections to insure full coverage. The summer I spent on an archaeological dig paid off in terms of what to do. Sure, of my parameters, I began a careful sweep of the snow and then checked the earth for footprints, clothing, Esaugetuh's pipe, animal remains, or anything that might suggest what happened to him. I spent the better half of the day on my hands and knees carefully marking out the smaller sections. Darkness forced me to stop. Disappointment was my reward for the day's efforts. Snow was gently falling. I hoped it wouldn't accumulate. It would just compound my search tomorrow. Sleep was fitful and once or twice, I thought I heard the purring of a cat.

The cawing of a crow announced the breaking dawn. Fortune smiled upon me; the trees had provided a shelter for the area and a great deal of fresh snow had not reached the ground. However, enough had to allow me to again note the prints of a cougar and the place where it had bedded down, right next to my tent. Has it replaced the eagle as my totem?

A strange phenomenon to say the least. Only time would reveal its intent. Its presence didn't threaten me but I did load the shotgun as a precaution. I also laid out an offering to its spirit as well as to its stomach. I chewed a left over biscuit and helped it down with hot coffee. Perhaps later in the day, I would look for some edibles within the forest to supplement my own food supply. I owe gratitude to Esaugetuh for those lessons.

The search was slow going and by day's end, I had found nothing to indicate anything about Esaugetuh. The flame in the center of the circle of seven stones had gone out yet the stones remained warm. Reluctant to move them I left them as they were. One more spoke of my seven-foot wheel remains. It will have to wait until tomorrow.

Sometime during the very early morning hours, one hell of a roar woke me. Grabbing the shotgun I cautiously peered out of the tent. Once again, the fire was burning in the circle of seven stones and I could vaguely see two massive figures thrashing around on its far side. A flashlight showed me the cougar on top of a large bear. Enormous balls of fur flew through the air as the cougar ripped into the bear frantically searching for the jugular vein. The bear, sensing its terrible danger, flung itself against a large tree in an effort to dislodge the cat. The cat fell to the ground and as the bear readied itself for revenge on the helpless cat; I fired. It wheeled around and I fired again. For an eternity, it stood perfectly still then swayed and fell to the ground.

I loaded the gun again and cautiously approached the bear. It was dead. The ground quickly drank its blood. I went to the cougar not knowing if it was alive or not. It was alive but obviously badly hurt. It might have crushed ribs and an injured animal can be deadly. But the sight and smell of the fired gun could cause it to make one last heroic effort to defend itself. Placing the gun against another tree, I returned to the cougar and slowly knelt by its side.

"Easy fella." I said, "You saved my life now it's my turn to return the favor."

Ever so slowly, I laid both of my hands on its rib cage and gradually moved them up and down the full length of his side. Its breathing steadied and its eyes calmed as death left. Once again, I realized I had automatically placed my right hand on top of my left. As the heat built, I felt a change in the cougar. It raised its head and licked my hand, got up and went to the bear, sniffed it, growled, and gave it a swipe. Satisfied that the bear was dead, the cougar moved off some distance, laid down, and began to clean itself. I picked up my gun and went back to my tent. The fire in the circle of seven stones was out. Apollo in his golden chariot was chasing the night across the sky. The long orange-red tendrils trailing high above the treetops foretold the arrival of another beautiful day and hopefully with it, a better day in my search.

The dawn showed that the fight had wrecked the entire area where I had been searching. Shaking my head in disgust, I looked over the area. I saw something glisten. I picked it up. It was Esaugetuh's medicine pouch. The sliver inlay had caught my attention.

I tied it around my neck. A shiver raced through me and I turned. The cougar was gone. I went over to the dead bear and it was then that I noticed its badly scarred face. Burned. Was it the same bear that had attacked Esaugetuh and me while we were on the Skagit River in Washington? He had said it would hunt us down. Had it killed Esaugetuh? More questions and still no answers.

There was no use in continuing to search the ground. The fight had made an absolute mess of the area. It would take a forensic team to sift through it. The bear had to be disposed of in some way. Before doing anything else, I felt it necessary to make an offering to the Spirits, an apology for having to kill the crazed bear.

I cleared away the debris from around the circle of seven stones. In its center, I laid seven braids of sweet grass, each pointing outward, and forming the spokes of a wheel. At their center, I built a small teepee of sweet grass. Then I added seven strands of the bear's fur. Looking around the area, I found seven strands of the cougar's hair and then I added seven strands of my own hair. I waited and waited. Nothing happened.

Then I remembered Esaugetuh's medicine pouch tied around my neck. I carefully opened it, removed a pinch of its contents, and sprinkled it over the sweet grass.

Instantly it burst into flames and with it my prayers of gratitude. I continued to sit there giving my body and spirit time to become one with my surroundings. A sense of Esaugetuh flooded my consciousness and I knew he had been here. I felt warm and safe. Perhaps reassured is a better word?

"Hello, the camp. We heard shots," broke my tranquil moment.

"Say, don't I know you?" said the second man.

"Yes. We've met before. I had to shoot that crazed bear.

"Hmm. Must be that crazy bear we've been hearing about. Attacked a couple of hikers awhile back," said the ranger.

"It appears to have been burned at one time. That would make it crazy." I offered.

"Could be. Mind telling me what you are doing out here?"

"I've been searching for something," I replied.

"And what might that something be?" said the other man.

"Still looking for your wallet?" the ranger said.

"Yes... that's it ... my wallet."

"Well, Mr. Esaugetuh you should have checked in with me. I have it. Stop by and you can claim it." The ranger replied.

After they left I returned to my searching the area to determine the direction of the cougar. Whether I wanted it or not our lives were now connected. The paw prints lead north. Not long into my hike, I heard a low growl. The closer I got to a thicket the fiercer the growl became. I stopped within eight feet of the thicket, sat down Indian style, and waited. Just its head appeared. We looked at one another.

"I've come to see if you are okay and to thank you for saving my life."

It wasn't a growl but more of a grunt. Then I heard it, the slow deliberate purring that I had heard for two nights. Contented that the animal was okay and that there was a peace between us I returned to my camp. Darkness was fast approaching and I still had no real idea as to what happened to Esaugetuh.

I brought a blue light and some luminal to help me in my search. They might show bloodstains or footprints not normally visible to the naked eye. I might get some indication if Esaugetuh had walked out of the area or if he had been injured and carried out. It was a long shot. A year and a half had passed since we were here. Or was it two years? Time is a strange bedfellow these days.

"Damn! Nothing. Not even the footprints of the rangers who had originally found me."

Disappointed , I decided to call it quits. I passed the blue light over a small area one more time. I stopped. Held the light steady. There was a slight impression in the dirt.

Kneeling down, I slowly I blew away the leaves. Gradually a full heel print showed and I knew it was Esaugetuh's. He always wore moccasins. The question is when did he make it. While we were looking for the sacred stones? Or was it made during or after my vision quest?

Using a regular flashlight, I examined the indentation, looking to see how much it had filled in. If there was a small amount of dirt in the deepest part of the footprint, then it was not new. Esaugetuh had taught me that while we were in the deep woods.

My heart pounded as I forced myself to be careful in clearing the dirt about three feet in front of the heel print.

"Hot damn!" I shouted.

A full print and then a second. Both lead away from the center and toward the north. I followed the footprints beyond the clearing and then lost them. I also noted a set of cougar tracks beside his. Not following but walking along with him.

I wonder if it's the same cougar?

At least I now know that he had left here on his own, but a couple of things still bothered me. First, was his medicine bag. He never was without it. Second, was the existence of his wallet. In all the time we were together, I never saw him with a wallet. Strange that the ranger kept the wallet all this time.

***

After breaking up camp and trekking back to the Cherokee, I went to see about the wallet. It was a well-used tan leather single fold and contained no money. It did contain a mutilated driver's license, a piece of paper with several addresses on it but no names attached to them, and a second piece of paper with a number written on it.

"Sorry about no money being left in it."

"No problem. Whoever it was is more than welcome to it. Glad they could make use of it."

"I appreciate that. What I mean to say is I'm appreciative of the fact that you aren't angry. A couple of hundred is a lot of money. Many folks would be hopping mad," the ranger said as I got back into the Cherokee.

Once out of sight of the rangers' station, I pulled off to the side of the road and stopped. Because I didn't know how much money was in the wallet, I hadn't mentioned it but the ranger knew. Guess I know who got the money. Of more interest to me was the list of nameless addresses, the piece of paper containing the number, and the driver's license. I took out the wallet and began to re-examine it. As I did so, I felt a small bulge on the inside, just beneath an emblem sewn on the outer flap.

Closer examination revealed the outline of a key. I tried dislodging it but to no avail. Then I realized that the emblem with its stitching was holding it in place. I cut the stitching and removed the key. It appeared to be a key to a locker. A flashing light reflected in my rearview mirror brought my examination to a halt. It was the ranger.

He got out of his car and came up to me. "Can we talk?" he asked.

"Sure," I said as I got out of the jeep.

"Look. I—, I 'm not sure how to say this."

"Well, the best way is just spit it out. Saves time that way."

The ranger's tanned face turned to a greenish hue. Small beads of sweat formed just beneath his hat.

Breathing hard, he blurted, "I took the money."

"I figured you did. Is that why you kept the wallet all this time?"

"Yeah. I figured I could explain and tell the person I'd pay him back. Man, this is harder than when I popped the question to my wife. I haven't got that amount of cash on hand right now but I'll pay you back. My wife was having a baby and I needed some quick cash."

"How much did you really take?"

"There were ten one-hundred dollar bills. Don't you. . ."

"And your wife and baby? How are they?"

"The wife's doing okay but she has taken it pretty hard that our son is blind. Like I said, I'll pay you back," he answered as he shook my hand. "Man, you hand is sure hot. You got one of those hand heaters?"

Ignoring his question about my hand I asked, "Did you try to track down any of those addresses?"

"No! Figured it wouldn't be any use since there were no names attached. Don't you know who they are? And the money? You didn't know how much was in the wallet. You better explain, mister. And begin by telling me who you really are."

"The wallet belonged to the man who was with me back when you found me."

"Hmm. And just who is this man? There was no one around when we rescued you. Where is this friend of yours now?"

"His name is Esaugetuh and I am his adopted son. The name's Adam. I don't know where he is. That's why I came back here. I thought I could find out where he went or what happened to him."

"You never did explain what you were doing in the woods, sitting around a dead fire pit, bare-assed naked."

"I came there to go on my vision quest. Esaugetuh was my guide. Don't suppose you could put these addresses into your computer and see what you get?"

"Come on back to my office and I'll see what I can find out. You won't say anything about the money, will you? I will pay him back."

"Don't worry. I'm sure he would've given you the money had he known your need." I replied.

The ranger pulled his vehicle by me, turned around, waved, and head back to his office. I climbed back into the jeep and just sat there.

Actually, I thought, I don't know what Esaugetuh would have done about the money. He was kind and respectful but I had no knowledge of his generosity at least not until his letter turning over his vast wealth was delivered to me.

Questions about that continually rear their heads. I feel it isn't generosity or charity on his part, nor is it because he loved me that he left me a fortune. My gut tells me there's an incompleteness, something that he didn't finish— something he wants me to finish for him. That creates an obligatory situation and I'm not sure I like that. At the same time, I know if I had not pursued him, traveled with him, sat at his feet, and listened to his wisdom I wouldn't feel this way. He used to tell me to seek a balance, to harmonize my body, mind, and spirit. He'd say, "Change your perspective and your perception, then you'll see, you'll understand."

***

I turned the jeep around and followed the ranger back into town. At his office, I handed him the list of addresses. Instead of going to his computer, he picked up the phone, punched in a number. Speaking in a hushed voice, with his back to me didn't ease my suspicions about him.

"Who was that you just called?"

"A friend of mine, an FBI agent. He says he'll run the addresses and get back to me."

"How long is that going to take?"

"Can't say for sure. You want some coffee. Fresh made."

"Sure. Is there a photographer here who can enlarge and enhance old photos? I'd like to get a better look at the photo on the driver's license."

"Yeah, down the street two blocks. On your left, Wiley's Photos," the ranger said, handing off a steaming cup of coffee.

"Thanks."

"Don't you recognize the man in the photo? You said you were his adopted son. Surely, you'd know if that was your father," the ranger said, stepping closer to look at the license I held out to him.

"That's just the point. I'm not sure that it is, at least not the man I know as Esaugetuh. Don't you think it strange that this license is old? Seems to me there would be one that's more current."

"Hmm. Maybe . . ."

The phone rang. The FBI agent had matched the addresses to names. I didn't recognize any of them.

Further questioning of the ranger revealed where and when the wallet had been found, and what shape it was in when found. Somewhat to my surprise, someone found it on a trail some distance from the Cathedral of Trees.

On my way back to the woods, I dropped the license off at the photographer. Once I got to the trail, I was still unsure of what might be there or even what I was looking for. That sure didn't make my search any easier. Three things remained clear to me: One was that I found Esaugetuh's medicine and second I knew he left the campsite, and third, he left on his own with a cougar was walking along with him.

My search along the trail proved fruitless. I stopped back at the photographers and his work was more productive. With the help of computer enhancement, he produced a relatively clear image.

"This the guy you are looking for? Ted told me you were looking for your father."

"Ted?"

"Yeah, the ranger. He called me."

"There might be some similarity but I still am not sure if this is the man I know as Esaugetuh."

I paid the photographer and then went back to the ranger's office. There, I asked him to fax the photo to his friend in the FBI to see if they had anything in their files. That search also produced nothing. They didn't make a match-up.

On my way out the door at the ranger's office, an attractive woman carrying a small child was hurrying up the walkway. I nodded and went on to my jeep, but before I got to the jeep, the ranger called me back.

"Like you to meet my wife and son. Ain't he something else?"

The ranger's pride and smile revealed a great deal about him.

"May I," I said reaching out to take the little boy. "He's about two?"

"Yes, today is his birthday," the ranger's wife said.

I rubbed my right hand over his head and he smiled. As I pulled my hand away, he reached up, grabbed it, and held on. A slight frown crossed his brow.

"I thought you said your son was blind. If so, how was he able to tell where my hand was and grab it?"

The ranger held up a finger and his son reached for it.

"My god," the ranger said, tears flowing down his tanned face.

The ranger's wife took back her son, held him close to her. The boy reached for her necklace and pulled and it fell to the floor. He began to wiggle and wanted down. As soon as he was on the floor, he went after the necklace.

"How is it that when you rubbed my son's head he could suddenly see? Who are you?"

"I told you, the name's Adam. Guess you better change doctors."

"You did this. You gave my baby sight. How can we ever thank you?"

"You already have," I said and walked out the door.

I now have a list of seven addresses and names to match them. They would be a start. So— it begins all over again.

CHAPTER 3 - JESSE CHRISTEN

**I know that people only seem to live when they live for themselves,
and that it is by love for others that they really live.
Tolstoy**

I decided to check the local bus depot. The key looked like a locker key. It was just a hunch. As it turned out it was not a good one. I returned to my hotel, feeling tired and more confused than ever, took advantage of the hotel's sauna.

The room was large enough for several people. It's walls were of eucalyptus, except for the entrance, which was made of glass doors. Wooden benches lined up along the inner walls with a row of hooks to hang a robe or towel.

A long steam would be enjoyable. I had time to look around while relaxing in its warm, soothing vapors. Directly opposite the glass doors was a bank of lockers. My eyes zeroed in on the numbers. Right in front of me was the same number as on the key. I jumped up, wrapped a large white Turkish towel around me, and hustled out of the sauna.

I quickly I opened the plastic container hanging around my neck, fished out the key, and tried it. The locker door made that familiar click. I pulled and the door opened.

"I'll be damned," I said, aloud.

A black duffel bag filled the cavity of the locker. I hesitated for a minute, then removed it. My comfort level had changed from one of relaxed reverie to one of apprehension. Long ago, I had learned to heed my inner warnings. I decided to return to my room before opening the duffel bag.

While I was getting off the elevator, I saw two men leaving my room. I ducked into one of those alcoves that have ice, snacks, and sodas. I waited until I no longer heard the whir of the other elevator and made a note of the floor where it stopped.

My stuff, thrown all over the place, made a huge mess in my room. The intruders even slashed my tube of toothpaste, smearing its contents all over the bedspread. Whatever they wanted it wasn't my money because my clip with a couple hundred dollars was still on top of the dresser. My billfold was on the bed, ripped apart but nothing was missing. Credit cards, license, list of names and addresses were all there.

After bolting the door I showered down, dressed, and then opened the black bag. It contained several thousand one hundred dollar bills. A quick estimate would make it nearly a half million dollars. How did these two guys know I had the key to the locker? It had to have been the key they were looking for. After cleaned up the room as best as I could I decided against calling the desk to check out and I also decided not to use the jeep Cherokee. If these two men knew my room number, they might also know the vehicle I was driving.

Using my cell phone, I called a cab and then slipped out without paying my bill. The cabby dropped me off at another hotel. As soon as he was out of sight, I called another cab and left that hotel, headed for another car rental and rented a Porsche. I felt I might need a fast car. A phone call to my former hotel authorized the payment for my room and I asked them to pick up the jeep and return it to the rental agency at the airport. I then headed southeast toward Virginia City. It was in that area that the first person on my list of seven lived. It took some time to locate the place because it was several miles off the main road. The rough dirt road brought me face to face with a woebegone singlewide trailer probably built back in the 60's. Sagebrush, thistles, cacti, and scrub pine dotted the landscape.

A large barking dog announced my arrival. Before I could heave my body out of the car, a tall dark skinned man, carrying a shotgun greeted me.

" What you want?"

"I'm looking for Jesse Christen," I replied. "Are you him?"

"I ain't saying I am and I ain't saying I'm not. What you want him for?"

"If you're Jesse I want to ask you some questions about a friend of mine."

A young woman with a small child in her arms appeared behind the man.

"Who is it, Jesse?"

"The name's Adam, a friend of Esaugetuh."

"Why didn't you say so? Come in. We're about to have supper. Ain't got much but we'd be right pleased to share it with you," the woman said.

The man stepped aside to let me exit the car. Inside, several wooden boxes made up the sum total of their furniture. Four bowls made of dried cactus leaves and hand-made wooden spoons lay on a large wooden box. In its middle, a loaf of homemade bread waited. Three small children huddled in a corner on a tattered blanket that served as their bed. I could see to the end of the trailer and into what must have been the man and woman's room. No bed, just a pile of blankets. Despite its total poverty, it was immaculately clean.

A bean soup with bread broken into small pieces was served. The three children in the corner watched every spoonful of soup that passed my lips. I was eating their supper. I could see the hunger in their eyes. I stopped eating, too full of guilt to eat anymore and at the same time overcome by their generosity. The totality of the situation reminded me of Tolstoy's *What Men Live By*.[4] I was the man taken in, a stranger from another world, and shared in whatever it was they had.

The woman fed the remaining food to her three older children, the oldest not quite five. Then sat down, giving her nipple to the infant. Jesse, squatting on the floor, pulled out his pipe; a clay pipe just like the one Esaugetuh always smoked. He noticed me looking at the pipe and misunderstanding my interest, offered it to me. I remembered Esaugetuh telling me if a man offers you a pipe, smoke it. Not to do so would be an offense. I accepted the pipe; took a hit, and returned it to Jesse, turning the stem to face my host.

"Where did you get that pipe?" I asked.

"Esaugetuh gave it to me. Said it would bring peace to my soul."

"And does it?"

"I used to think it did, but then I've smoked all the tobacco he gave me. Now I smoke dried sage. It's just not the same."

"I have some of his tobacco I'll give you. It's Kinnikinnick."

"He said that a man would come by and say he was a friend. Said I would know the Biblical reference. I don't recall the name Esaugetuh as being in the Bible. What does it mean?" Jesse said.

"Esaugetuh means Master of Breath. How long ago was he here and how did you meet him?"

"It was sometime before Mary and me got married. Maybe seven or eight years ago. I had me an old Ford truck then and I was coming back from a night in town. It was one of them real dark nights and with only one headlight, it was hard to see. I nearly ran over him. He was just standing there in the road, looking straight at me with those blue eyes of his. They seemed to glow and that's how I knew they were blue. Nearly scared me to death. Fact is I ain't been the same since."

"Jesse, excuse me. I want to get something from my car. I'll be right back."

Outside, I reached into the duffel bag, pulled out several stacks of the one-hundred dollar bills, and grabbed the remains of the supplies from my camping in the Cathedral of Trees.

When I gave Jesse the money, he refused it.

"Can't take money from a stranger, especially since it ain't been earned."

"This money was given to me to be delivered to you. Your name was on a list left to me by Esaugetuh."

His woman quietly wept. He turned his head, too embarrassed to speak.

"Look, I better get going. It's not a good idea for me to remain any longer. It might be dangerous for you and your family."

"Nonsense. We know how to run off intruders. Done it plenty a time. You got trouble, it's our trouble."

Sleep was fitful. Several times, I groaned and Jesse would gently lay his hand on my shoulder and whisper "You okay?" Once assured that I was he went back to his watching. At some point just before dawn, I heard the far off squeal of tires and then the hum of a motor. I got up from the floor. Jesse was gone. I peered out the window and could see car lights fast approaching the trailer. A flash and then the roar of a shotgun blast. The children began to cry. Their mother was nowhere in sight. A second gunshot told me she was out there with her husband. I bolted out the door and ran to my car. Frantically I searched through my bag to find my gun.

"They've gone. Won't be back," she said. "Jesse and me put the fear of God into 'em."

"You sure you didn't steal all that money?" It was Jesse.

"I didn't steal it. It's mine. There's something you need to know."

Inside I explained how Esaugetuh was missing and that I was trying to find him. I told them about the wallet, the key to the locker, and the men at the hotel.

"Well, I don't know where Esaugetuh is but I can tell you about the wallet. It must have been a couple of years ago. He stopped by. He paid me to take it over to Lake Tahoe and toss it on a certain trail. He told me not to look in it. And I didn't."

"I don't understand all of this business but one thing I do know and that is you must not go into Reno to spend this money. Don't spend it all at once. You understand?" I said.

Jesse nodded and the woman went to her children. I continued to question Jesse about the remaining names on my list. He knew none of them. As I left, I handed him a bag of Kinnikinnick for his pipe.

Going back to Reno was not a good idea so I headed south to Las Vegas. There I returned the car and caught a flight to Phoenix.

Marrie Copa, the next person on my list, lived north of there, near a place called Sedona in Arizona's high desert.

CHAPTER 4 - MARRIE COPA

**This being human is a guest house. Every morning is a new arrival. Be grateful for whoever comes, because each has been sent as a guide form beyond.
Rumi**

Sedona, among other things, is one of those New Age Spiritual centers. The drive north from Phoenix was uneventful. I found Marrie in an apartment complex for the elderly, located in a small town not far from Sedona.

She didn't hesitate to invite me in when I knocked on her door.

Very old and wheel chair bound, she barely spoke above a whisper. Her thin weather-worn skin accentuated her frail bony body. Her thin hair, streaked with gray was in a single braid that hung over her left shoulder. Almost immediately, she corrected my pronunciation of her name.

Young man, if you are going to call me by my name pronounce it correctly. My name is Mar-rie. Not like Mary."

"Yes, grandmother. Thank you for correcting me."

Calling her grandmother was within the tradition of Native Americans. Esaugetuh's admonition about being respectful still hounded my conscience.

It was very difficult trying to talk to her because of her gravelly voice, which faded in and out like a bad radio signal. Sometimes her words were almost slurred. The strain began to agitate me as we sat there drinking some kind of horrible tasting tea.

What's her connection to Esaugetuh, I thought.

"Something' wrong with your side?" she asked.

"What? No, nothing. Just a catch," I replied wondering how she knew it was bothering me.

The furniture, sparse as it was, was very old. Two chairs, a small table, two lamps, only one on, and an old TV. My eyes came back to the small table. It had been there all along. I was so agitated by the old woman's raspy voice, I hadn't noticed it, a picture of Esaugetuh.

"The photo on the stand. Is he a relative of yours?" I asked as I got up to get a better look.

"He's—."

I blurted, "When was the last time you saw him."

The little apartment was very warm, suffocating. I could barely focus.

Shit, I thought, she's drugged me.

I woke up in a hospital with an assortment of machines attached to me.

"What happened? How'd I get here? Where's Marrie Copa?" I asked a nurse who had entered the room.

"Evidently you fainted, struck your head. Your grandmother must have called 911 before she collapsed."

"Collapsed?"

"She's in the cardiac unit. The doctor will be with you shortly."

And to think I thought she had drugged me. I wish I understood the irritation that comes over me at times.

A knock on my door interrupted my thoughts. It was the doctor.

"You doin' okay?"

"Why don't you tell me?" There I go again, I thought.

"Can't say. I'd like to keep you over night to monitor you and if there are no further complications, you can go home tomorrow. By the way, when did you have a rib removed?"

"Rib removed? I've never had a rib removed. I've never been in a hospital except when I was born."

"Hmm! Well, you have a missing rib in your right side. Your grandmother said you had a pain in your side. Mind telling me about it?"

I started to say she wasn't my grandmother but changed my mind.

I've had it quite a while. I just thought it was a little gas. Nothing serious. You sure I have a rib missing?"

"Yes. The x-rays show a rib is missing. Yet there is no scar tissue anywhere."

"How is grandmother? I need to go to her."

"She's suffering from congestive heart failure. Even though she's very frail, she should be okay with the proper medication and diet. I'll have an orderly wheel you up to see her. Don't stay too long. Both of you need to rest."

"Why is she in a wheel chair?" I asked.

"I don't know. She's not one of our patients so I don't have any records on her but her feet are badly deformed. I suspect she has a degenerative bone disease."

"Can anything be done?"

"I don't know. We'd have to have another specialist look at her. That'd be quite expensive. Do you know if she has insurance besides Medicare?"

"No I don't but whatever the cost there's money to pay. Call whatever specialists you need. I'll be in town for a few more days. I'd appreciate a report."

The orderly wheeled me into her room. She looked so pale, so helpless laying there with her eyes closed. I felt guilty because I was agitated by her speech.

She sensed my presence and said, "I wondered when you'd come. Feel guilty, do you?"

"As a matter of fact yes I do. I was totally disrespectful. I'm sorry," I said as I indicated I wanted the orderly to leave. Once he was out of sight, I took both of her hands into mine. She knew what I was doing.

"It won't make any difference," she whispered. "I'm too old."

"Don't talk. Just relax."

"If I relaxed any more I'd be dead," she teased.

I was glad to see she had a sense of humor. As frail as she was, she wasn't morose.

The heat came into my hands and began to flow to hers. She smiled and gradually dosed off to sleep. I leaned over her, placed my right hand over heart. The heat caused her to stir and groan.

I remained at her bedside the rest of the day. Late, that afternoon she woke up and was ready to sit up and eat. She ate with gusto. I wondered then if she had enough money to buy proper foods as well as any medication she needed. Another person who needs some financial help.

Wonder if that's what this list is all about, I thought. Marrie's voice got my attention.

"You wanted to know about the photograph on my table?"

"Yes, if you feel like talking for a while."

"Well, there ain't all that much to tell. He's a relative on my father's side, a medicine man, lives some place in Canada. Not sure where. He came to see me awhile back. Gave me that picture."

"How long ago? Can you be more specific?"

"Oh dear, I'm not really sure. Maybe two, three years ago."

"Is that all?" I asked unable to conceal my disappointment.

"I hear he's been married several times and as I recall there ain't any children."

"What happened to his wives?"

"If there were any, I don't rightly know, but I reckon he simply outlived 'em. He's very old. A lot older than me and I'm old."

"Did he tell you anything about himself?"

"No, not really. Said he was on a journey. Gave me some of his medicine and said a man would come into my life and he'd have very powerful medicine."

"Did he name this man?"

"Said his name would be Adam, a man of the earth. You're him, ain't ya?"

"I am that I am," I said and this time there was somebody there.

Just as I was about to ask another question another doctor came in. He checked the machines, listened to the Marrie's heart, and then shook his head in disbelief.

"I can't believe it. There is such a change in the readings on the monitor. Her heart, according to the readings, is in fine shape. I want to change monitors to make sure there's not an error in the readings. Also, I'd like to do an echocardiogram. If everything is okay there then I don't see why she can't go home. Everything seems normal but I still don't understand the change."

"No more tests," Marrie said.

"We just want to make sure you are okay," said the doctor.

"I'm fine. I want to go home."

"What about her feet? Can you do something? I'd like to see her out of that wheel chair," I said.

"You can have a podiatrist examine her feet. If you like, I'll make an appointment for her."

"Great! I appreciate that. I'll make sure she's on time. Now if you'd tell me how to get to the hospital cashier."

I checked myself out, paid the bills, and called for a taxi. Like, two escapees, we were soon on our way back to Marrie's apartment. There, I asked her to look at the remaining five names on my list. She didn't get the change. Her telephone rang.

Incident creates the connection between Jesse and Esaugetuh; Marrie Copa's connection is blood line. Both were expecting me but how do I fit into all of this? What is it that I am to find out? Why does he have me looking for these people? Why didn't I know I had a rib missing? Strange that my parents never mentioned it nor any doctor that ever examined me. Questions and more questions.

I must have dozed in my chair. Marrie poking me with a cane awakened me.

"I've been thinking," she said, "I've got a tin box, the kind they used to pack fish in. It's full of old pictures and other mementos in the storage area of the building. Maybe you can get it out and you'll find some things of interest."

"We haven't eaten yet?" I said ignoring her comments about pictures.

"No, but I'll have something ready as soon as you get that tin box. You go down the hall, up to the third floor and it's the third door on your left. Here's the key."

Dutifully I went to get the box. There were pieces of furniture, other boxes of stuff, bags full of magazines, books. What an assortment of junk! The lack of a light in the room didn't make it any easier. Finally, I found the tin box and returned to the apartment.

Marrie had tea and biscuits ready and by the looks of them, she had had them a long time. Being sure that I couldn't drink another cup of her tea, I said, "Let's go out to eat. You feel up to it?"

Her eyes lit up.

"Let me fix my face. Can't be seen in public with a handsome stud while I look a mess. Get this infernal hospital identification tag off my wrist."

During lunch, she told me about her three husbands, a son that was killed in the war, a twin sister whom she thought was dead. Esaugetuh was her only living relative. I appreciated the fact she referred to him as still living.

We made a stop at a local grocers on our way back to the apartment. By then Marrie was tired and her much needed nap gave me the opportunity to call Running-water and touch base with him.

He had located Esaugetuh's home, the bank, the office buildings, but no information as to where Esaugetuh might be or if he was dead or alive. Said he was running out of leads. I quickly filled him in on my own doings. Immediately, he wanted to join me, and since the encounter with the men in Reno and at Jesse's place, I felt it might be a good idea.

"Look," I said, "There is still the question of how those men knew about the key, the money, and me. If they could track me to Jesse's, maybe they have tracked me to Marrie's and she could be in danger. Let me know if you can get a flight."

"Give me a half hour and I'll call you back," Running-water said.

"Hold on. What's the matter with me? Use the Gulfstream Jet Esaugetuh turned over to me. Isn't it there in Montreal? Get me the number of the pilot and where its housed and I'll order it up for you."

I called, identified myself as Adam, and much to my surprise it was 'yes sir' all over the place. The Gulfstream would be ready for Running-water. Instead of waiting until tomorrow, I would pick him up tonight.

During our evening meal, which I had cooked, it became obvious

that one of Marrie's problems was lack of proper nourishment. I made a mental note to see about meals on wheels for her. I glanced up at her and caught her giving me the once over.

She began to giggle and a blush colored her wrinkled face.

"You make a good wife," she teased.

"Are you proposing?"

"Believe me if I were younger I would. You'd make good babies," she said reaching across the table and patting my hand.

"Now, behave yourself, " I said, picking up her hand, and feigning a kiss. " Marrie," I continued, " I have to go to Flagstaff to pick up a friend who is flying in from Canada. While I'm gone, I don't want you to go to the door, stay away from windows. Don't answer the phone. It's very important that you do as I ask."

"Don't worry. You in some kind a trouble?"

"No, but there are those who might harm you if they knew I was here. So, will you do as I ask?"

"Yes."

"Good. It will be very late when I get back. You will know when—."

"Yes, I'll know."

***

During the short trip to the airport, I had an uneasy feeling and kept an eye on the rear view mirror. Thankfully, it was uneventful. With time to kill before Running-water arrived, I decided to get a massage to relieve the tension in my neck and shoulders. That helped but it still didn't shake off the uneasiness that was engulfing me.

Everyone became a person of interest. As they walked past my table in one of the cafés, I speculated about who and what they were. My cell phone vibrated just as my attention focused on a particularly attractive young woman.

"Man you won't believe this plane. The seats, no--chairs, are of fancy leather and swivel. Each has a round table with a pop-up computer/television monitor. This baby must be worth millions."

"Everything is okay, then?"

"Yes. Well, no. The attendant is a real fox. She was all over me until she called me Adam and I told her that wasn't my name. Talk about frigid. The same thing happened when the pilot came back. Real solicitous. When he learned my name, he stopped talking and walked away."

"Strange. When I talked to the pilot it was yes sir this and yes sir that. I've had the jitters ever since I left Marrie's. Stay alert."

"Roger that," Running-water said.

It would be about forty-five minutes before touchdown. He would have to clear customs since he was coming in from Canada, and then go through a security check.

I made the mistake of assuming the plane would be landing at one of the regular gates. It took a page to direct me to the correct gate. Of course, it was at the other end of the airport. Running-water was the first off the plane. After a quick hello and a handshake, I waited for the pilot and flight attendant to come through the gate. They were about to walk right by Running-water and would have had I not spoken to them.

"I'm Adam."

They stopped in their tracks nearly tripping over one another.

"Yes, Sir. Glad to meet you, Sir." The pilot said extending his hand.

Ignoring his hand I said, "I want the plane re-fueled, placed in a hanger, and put tight security on it. I want a complete lock down."

"Yes, Sir. I'll tend to it as soon as I check into the hotel," the pilot said.

"No, you will do that now. Do you have a relief pilot and navigator available?"

"Yes, but they're not located here. They will have to fly in."

The pilot's voice now cold and agitated didn't set well with me.

"Good. Get them here and tell them to stand by for further orders."

"Sir?"

" Once you have this done call me at this number," I said as I handed him a card. "That's it for now. Get your eight hours. I'll be in touch. And as for you, miss," I said turning to the flight attendant, "I strongly suggest you wear a more appropriate uniform. I prefer something in light blue. Buy a couple and be prepared to fly out on short notice."

"What's wrong with what I have on? These aren't cheap, ya know," she snapped.

"A see-through blouse, no bra, and a skirt up to your ass is not the kind of professional image I want on my plane. Have I made myself understood?"

"I am a professional and nobody but nobody—." Bursting into tears she never finished her sentence.

She paused, sniffed a couple of times.

"Okay, so I'm a hooker hired for this trip. You don't have to be so cold and mean?"

"Who hired you and why?" I said, reaching for her arm.

She wasn't quick enough to pull away. I Ran my finger down her slightly up-turned nose and blew into her eyes.

She immediately relaxed.

"I don't know who hired me. All I know is my pimp told me where to go and how much to charge," she said.

"And how much was that?"

"One thousand big ones."

"I suppose you'll face some unpleasantness when you return ."

"Oh yeah. A whole bunch."

"Here's the thousand," I said handing her ten one hundred dollar bills."

She folded the bills, lifted her short skirt, and stuck them in her underwear. Every man's head turned as she swayed her way toward the exit. She stopped, turned.

"Thanks, Adam. I could have made it good for you, you know."

"Man, you 're something else. You were kind of harsh with her, weren't you?

"I really didn't mean to sound the way I did. Sometimes, I just get irritated, frustrated. I nearly went nuts with Marrie's gravelly voice. And that kind of thing is not like me."

"What do we do now?" Running-water said, grinning.

"Now what?"

"Just remembering another time you were irritated," Running-water said, as he gave me a poke.

"Okay, smart ass, just knock it off. We head back to Marrie's apartment. She has a box of old photos we can go through. We might find something there about Esaugetuh."

"How many people did you say were on your list?".

"Seven. I've seen two. Five to go."

"Who looked up the addresses for you?"

"The ranger back at Tahoe. Why?"

"Maybe that's how those two guys knew where you were and what you were after."

"No, I don't think so. The ranger didn't know I found the key. He had a friend in the FBI get the addresses. There might be some connection there," I said as we piled into the car.

We'd gone only a few miles on Route 17 when my old and all too familiar sickness hit me. This time with a renewed vengeance.

The car swerved as I struggled to focus. The car bounced along the berm. My head hit the steering wheel.

"Holly shit!" Running-water shouted, grabbing the steering wheel.

Giving it a hard pull, the car shot forward and back onto the road.

"Get your goddamn foot off the accelerator," Running-water yelled.

Sharp pain bore through my ankle. He kicked me again dislodging my foot from the accelerator. The car slowed as he eased it to the side of the road.

Running-water reached over me, turned off the ignition. We stopped.

"Man! You look like a piece a shit. What the hell's wrong with you? You could've gotten us killed," Running-water said, exiting the car.

I was aware of being pulled out of the car, dragged a few feet and then shoved back into the car. Everything seemed to be far away and in slow motion.

"Man! Your hands are red hot," Running-water said as he moved me around to fasten my seatbelt.

My hands were burning, yet, I was freezing. Uncontrollable spasms of shaking wracked my body.

I managed to give directions to Running-water and then tried to sleep even thou we had only a few miles to go.

Images of fire kept invading my consciousness. They were so strong that I felt the heat and smelled the smoke. The realism of the images woke me. I looked around and realized Running-water had slowed to get by a black sedan parked a building down from Marrie's apartment. It was nearly daylight and a light was on in the window of her apartment.

With Running-water's help, I managed to get up the steps to Marrie's apartment. She opened the door before we could even knock.

Marrie pointed to a chair and Running-water helped me to sit down.

"What happened?" Marrie said.

"Don't know. He got sick in the car and couldn't drive. I think he actually passed out. I'm Running-water."

" I guessed as much. Get his feet up on that stool, put this pillow behind him. I'll make some hot tea. You want some. It's fresh bought."

"Sure. May I help?"

"No. Kitchen's too small for two people. You know how to take a pulse reading? If you do, take his pulse."

Marrie brought the tea. She had laced it with a good shot of brandy. While I sipped my tea, she gave the tin box to Running-water to sort.

As the day progressed so did my illness. I floated in and out. The smell of food roused me and turned my stomach into a churn. Sometimes I was aware that Running-water making stacks of photos, papers, and stuff from Marrie's tin box.

By nightfall, he had gone through hundreds of old photographs, scraps of newspaper, pages from magazines, and a few letters. Running-water found a letter signed by Esaugetuh in which he detailed the directions to a healing place, a power place.

"I know this place. Powerful medicine there. You must leave now and be there when the sun first makes his appearance," Marrie said.

Rousing myself, I said, "Why? What's so important about this mountain?"

"You're Adam, man of the earth. It's there you must go to get your strength back. The earth there is sacred. Much power there."

"We better do as she says. You're really sick. In fact you look like hell," Running-water said.

"But I'm not an Indian. It probably wouldn't work for me," I said, forcing myself to stand.

I looked out the widow of Marrie's apartment and spotted the black car sitting along the curb. I recalled seeing it when we drove in. There appeared to be two people sitting in the front seat. That set off my inner voice, raising red flags. I wondered why they were still in the car.

"Running-water, hand me the car keys," I said.

"Man, you can't drive. Not like you are."

"Just give me the goddamn keys."

As soon as I had the keys, I pointed them out the window, pushed a button. The car exploded into a ball of fire. My vision had come true.

"My god, why'd you blow up the car?" Marrie said.

"The car had a remote starter. I've felt uneasy and thought it best to start ," I replied. "That black car made me even more suspicious."

"Damn good thing you were. We'd be burnt toast," Running-water said.

"We need to get to that car and see who's in it. Strange they haven't taken off or jumped out to see what's going on. They were then when we arrived this morning."

When we got to the car, each of us took a side and yanked the doors open. The two men were dead. Each had a small bloody spot on the back of the neck, just behind the lower part of the ear, and yet there were no bullet holes in the car windows.

"Those aren't bullet holes. Furthermore, there's no exit hole," Running-water said, as he looked closer at the driver.

"Really strange. Wonder what could have caused that kind of wound. These guys certainly didn't put up a struggle," I said.

Sirens announced the arrival of fire trucks, rescue, and police. There would be questions and I didn't want to answer any of them.

"Hey, ain't you Adam?" said one of the paramedics; "I took you to the hospital a couple days ago."

"I am. Can you tell me something about these two dead guys? What killed them?"

"No can do. That's up to the coroner. Say, you don't look too good. Maybe you better get in out of the night air."

"Yeah, you're right. I'll take him in right now," Running-water said as he took me by the arm and escorted me back to the apartment.

"What the hell you trying to do? I want to know how those men died," I growled at Running-water as he shut and locked the door to Marrie's apartment.

"Ask her. She knows, don't you old girl?"

"Is that true, Marrie? You know what killed those men?" I said.

"You have many friends that look out for you, Adam, man of the earth. Do not shun their help. The Spirits will not like it," Marrie said.

"You haven't answered my question, old lady. You owe me and you know it," I said.

My words had barely vaporized into the air when I felt the pain in my ribs. The pain was so severe I had to sit down. Evidently, that frightened Marrie because she began talking in her own language. I was about to say something when two burly looking men came in from her bedroom. Even Running-water backed up a couple of steps.

"They planted the bomb in your car. They are no more. That's all you need to know. There's a jeep in the alley behind this apartment. It's ready for you. Go! The police will soon begin a systematic search and questioning of each apartment," said the larger of the two men.

As we started down the back stairs, the other man handed me my duffel bag. Opening it, I quickly shoved a couple stacks of the money into his hand.

"Whoever you are, take care of Marrie."

CHAPTER 5 - HIGH DESERT

**If you know when to stop, you'll suffer no harm.
And in this way, you can last a very long time.**

Lao Tzu

The jeep had its own communication system, an air compressor, a
high lift jack, fire extinguisher, front tow hook, food, water, and other survival gear. Whoever the two men were, they had thought of everything. With Running-water behind the wheel, we headed northwest toward Prescott.

There we picked up 89A and drove until we came to the northwest corner of Verde Valley and Little Grand Canyon. At some point, we would be leaving the main road and heading into the Sycamore Creek area. The jeep would allow us to do the necessary crawling as we moved through tight washes and their large boulders.

Being concerned that we might miss the markers mentioned in Esaugetuh's letter, we decided to pull off and bed down for the night. A lot of years had passed since Esaugetuh had written that letter and we couldn't be sure if those markers were still there. Man, as well as nature, could have altered them thus making it impossible to tell where we were going. Nightfall complicated matters. Besides, I needed to rest. We ate a piece of jerky and downed a bottle of water before calling it a day.

For a time, it seemed all I did was dream of the time Esaugetuh pulled the Pigmy Rattler from my chest while I was at that motel in Florida. The song of its rattles was so clear that I opened my eyes. Once again, I was staring into the open mouth of a rattler. This time I felt no fear and it seemed to be speaking to me. There was an urgency about it.

Finally, I understood and it slithered away into the bush. Quietly I disengaged myself from my sleeping bag, grabbed my gun, and made a circle of the jeep. There I saw two men crouched. One seemed to be doing something beneath the jeep. I turned the flashlight on him. He let out a terrifying scream and began thrashing around on the ground; the other jumped up, ran a short distance, and keeled over.

The scream brought Running-water to his feet.

"Holy shit! What the hell's going on?"

"Don't know."

Both men were dead. Each had several fang marks on his neck. Flooding the area with the lights on the jeep, we continued to look around.

"Man, look at this." Running-water said, "I've never seen such a huge rattler in my life; Never heard of one being out this time of year either. It can't be much above 30 degrees."

I bent down to get a closer look. It was still alive but apparently exhausted by its vicious attack on the two men. There is no question that it intended to kill.

"Bring me some water," I said.

Pouring a small amount into the palm of my hand, I extended it to the snake. The snake's forked tongue flicked over the water several times and then it slithered away.

"Man, you are crazy. The rattler could have nailed you," Running-water said.

"It woke me up and it saved our lives. Better check under the jeep for a bomb."

There was one, but fortunately, for us; the man didn't get the chance to connect it. We found their car a short distance away, searched it and found only a map, a rental receipt. We then went back and made a search of the two men. Both men had driver's licenses from another state, credit cards and one had the same list of names that I did. On the same piece of paper was a different telephone number containing a Flagstaff prefix.

Something, I'll check later," I said, folding the paper and slipping into my pocket.

Running-water cleared the area of our footprints, Indian style. Then he brought up their car, punctured a hole in one of the tires, jacked up the car, and placed the two men beside the tire. Again, he swept the area clean and we left. He also made sure that we left no fingerprints.

His efficiency amazed me. He caught me watching him.

"What?"

"Nothing," I said. "It's nearly dawn. Guess we better hit the road."

Some miles from there, we left the main road again and headed through a wash toward Sycamore Creek. Normally there would be lush vegetation but at this time of year, snow was more likely the ground cover of choice.

Luck was with us. There wasn't any. No watercress and other flowering plants to please the eye. However, the Ponderosa pines, cacti and the towering red rocks, each, in turn, expressed their own beauty.

Running-water eased our way through several very tight washes where some large boulders scraped the side of the jeep. The hoodoos began to fascinate me. These vertical rock formations were millions of years old and I wondered how many people had worked their way up the face of some of them.

Coming out of my mind-wanderings and remembering the telephone number I had found on one of the dead men, I decided to call and see who answered.

Running-water stopped the jeep and I punched in the number. A woman answered the phone and I recognized her voice. The connection went dead.

"So we now have a Canadian connection. The person who answered the phone was none other than the woman on the Gulfstream," I said.

"Why didn't you confront her?" Running-water asked.

"She hung up or the connection was terminated."

"Maybe she was terminated," Running-water replied. "Too bad if she was; she was a fox."

He started the jeep and eased it along.

"Possibly. Her connection to the two back there might account for her coldness toward you when she found out you were not me," I said as we caught the air and I nearly tumbled out.

We had to stop once and use the high lift jack. Running-water sure knew what he was doing. I wasn't much help. I seemed to be getting weaker and weaker. I felt it might be time for my Spirit-Self to move on, yet something deep within me said otherwise.

My weakness made me feel euphoric at times and other times totally passive. It came in uncontrollable waves. I have had these episodes several times in the last few months. They seem to be progressively worse.

We had arrived at a stream.

"Now what? " Running-water said.

I ignored his question as I struggled to get out of the jeep. I hung on to the open door as I stripped off my clothes. Once in the icy water, I laid down. Its temperature not much above freezing. I rolled over, face down and felt severe pain as the water filled my ears. Fearing that I was drowning myself, Running-water jumped into the water, scooped me up, and dragged me out of the water.

Screaming at me, "What the hell are you doing? You gone crazy?"

"No. It's okay," I said gasping for air and shaking like the last leaf on a windblown tree. "Take me to the mountain and there make a sweat lodge."

The jeep made the climb with ease. We were nearly at 3000 feet and on sacred ground. Many spirits, holy beings seemed to be welcoming me. My whole body tingled as it felt the energy around me. I sensed their power and knew this was the place to construct a sweat lodge.

Running-water drew a circle about four feet from the center of a node, I had indicated. He drew a second inner circle and at its center, he dug a hole.

I sat down, tried to calm myself. I remembered another time when I had tried to pray and how difficult it was. Like then, I waited.

While I sat there, letting my thoughts take me wherever they wanted, Running-water constructed a crude sweat lodge using juniper, willow, and some sycamore branches. He covered these poles with a canvas tarp from the jeep.

Next, he brought several rocks for me to test for their warmth. When I was satisfied and had selected seven he built the fire and began to heat them. Once they were really hot, Running-water transferred them to the sweat lodge. Crawling inside, I laid seven braids of sweet grass soaked in water on top of the seven hot stones to help create steam, then some juniper on top of the sweet grass. I also added some angelica root to attract the good Spirits. Running-water, serving as the fire-keeper, kept the rocks hot throughout the night. I took no water or food. The steam and heat did their work. I asked the holy Spirits to heal me, to purify my being, and to make me whole once again.

Just before dawn, I crawled out of the sweat lodge and rubbed my entire body with rhyolite. [5] Once, rhyolite covered my body, I began my journey to the top of the mountain. Often I would slip and have to claw my way inch by inch back again.

"Daman it, Adam, let me help you," Running-water shouted.

"No. Stay where you are."

Blood oozed from my scraped knees; their skin hanging in shreds in some places. My chest hair was matted with drying blood from the deep scraps caused by my constant slipping and sliding.

I screamed. I was sure my testicles got crushed as I fell against a sharp rock. Death at the moment would have been most welcome.

Half crazed and not really knowing what I was doing I dragged myself the last few feet to the top, not far from the cement slab used by hang gliders, I forced myself to stand at its center. Through the remnants of early dawn, the sun focused its rays directly upon my quivering body already made red by the rhyolite and dried blood. A radiant cocoon engulfed me as the whole panorama revealed a glow of golden copper and orange, creating a typical Barry Goldwater photograph.

The heat penetrating every muscle and sinew of my naked body generated a new strength that rushed full force throughout my whole being. I looked to the heavens searching. I had no idea what I was looking for.

"What is it you want of me?" I cried out as I strained my eyes to see to the end of the universe.

Then it came into view, a great bald eagle circling closer and closer. I spread my arms out and upward in welcome. I heard its voice.

I answered, "I am that I am!" as my tears streaked the red rock's dust on my face.

I remained standing there absorbing the sun's strength and feeling the power of the mountain until the sun began to recede from its day-long journey across the vast Arizona sky.

I felt really well for the first time since my vision quest at Tahoe nearly three years ago. Like Moses of old, I came down off the mountain, not with a tablet of stone, but with a new strength and vigor. He too must have felt a new energy, a renewal of his spirit and soul.

Running-water gave me some much needed water at the same time ordering me to drink little and to drink slowly. As soon as I dressed, we dismantled the sweat lodge and made sure there were not hot coals left in the fire-pit. Following an old wagon trail, we began our descent into Mescal Canyon and eased our way back to civilization. We checked in at a motel.

A hot shower removed the rhyolite and food satisfied the emptiness in our guts. I again called the number I found on one of the dead men. This time a man answered the phone. It was the pilot.

"This is Adam. Where's the girl? I want to talk to her."

"Uh, she's uh in the shower." the pilot stammered.

"Go get her."

"She says she can't come to the phone right now."

"Get her. I paid for her. Tell her to get her sweet ass to the phone and do it now." I growled.

"Well, actually she's not here right now."

"Which is it? She's in the shower or not there?"

"She's not here."

"When she gets back tell her to be ready to fly out. Did you lock down the plane as I ordered?"

"Yes, sir."

"What security company did you use?"

"Not any. I just hired a couple of guys from here to guard the plane. Anything wrong with that?"

"No problem. I'll call back when I get back to the city, so stay put." I said as I hung up.

"We're going back?" Running-water said.

"Not until we have a changing of the guard and pilots. You know anybody who can fly a Gulfstream Jet?"

"No, but I know someone who might. Want me to find out?"

"Yes, but don't use the phone in here. Also, ditch this cell phone. I noticed a place just down the street that sells them. Go there, buy a new one, and sign up for a whole new service. Use this address." I said as I handed him a card. No credit cards. Use cash only. There's money in the bag."

"What's going on? You know something you're not telling me?" Running-water said as he unzipped the duffle bag." Holly shit! What the hell did you do, rob a bank? "

"That's the money that was stashed in the locker at the hotel. I used the key in Esaugetuh's wallet to open it. I figure the only way people know where I am is through my cell phone."

"Got it. Be right back."

While Running-water was gone, I tried to reconstruct the events that had taken place. That was the second attempt on my life. The half million dollars is certainly sufficient motivation for someone to track down and even kill me, but the pilot and the girl's involvement aren't ringing true. There must be some other connection.

"Change your perspective and perceptions."

"Is that you Esaugetuh? Where are you?"

"Use all the resources you have as well as those I've given you. There are forces that would destroy you, powerful forces that do not want you to exist."

"Esaugetuh! Where are you?"

Silence!

"What about Running-water?" I said. "He seems to be too conveniently available."

"Running-water is your soul-mate. He will die for you, if necessary." came the voice. "Change your perspective and your perceptions will change."

"Damn it, Esaugetuh. Show yourself and knock off this cat and mouse game."

"Haven't learned much have you?"

A shooting pain caught me in the ribs and I groaned. Just then, Running-water knocked at the door and I let him in.

"Who was that you were talking to?" he said as he shut and bolted the door behind him.

"Just talking out loud. Did you have any luck getting us a new pilot?"

"Yes. He'll bring his own navigator and will meet us at Marrie's.

"Great. We can go back to Flagstaff."

'Adam, I've been thinking," Running-water said. " It seems to me that we have two different issues here. First, the disappearance of Esaugetuh and second, the half million dollars. I don't think they are necessarily connected."

"There are several possibilities. What about the pilot and the girl? What's their connection? What's the connection among these seven people on the list? What is their connection to Esaugetuh? Seems to me they are."

"Okay."

"Are the people on list connected to the money or is it connected to the pilot and the girl? And what about the ranger and Esaugetuh's wallet?" I asked.

" You've missed one," Running-water said.

"Who?"

"You. Someone else may believe he should have been Esaugetuh's beneficiary."

"True. And another thing. We don't know how the money got in the locker, who put it there, or whose it really is for that matter. Yet, somehow I feel it was intended that I should locate the money."

"How's that?"

"Esaugetuh had the wallet thrown on the trail, knowing that I would return to Tahoe."

"Let's suppose for the moment that it's because you inherited all of Esaugetuh's money. Who besides you would have benefited from Esaugetuh's estate?" asked Running-water.

"I wish I knew. According to Marrie, he didn't have any children and no wife. Somehow, all of these are tied together. Find that connection and we'll have our answer."

"More likely it's Esaugetuh's medicine they're after. He was very powerful and that power is now yours whether you realize it or not. Let's be a little more cautious. They've nearly nailed you twice. You know the old saying, ' three times and you're out.' So, who's next on the list?"

"You have a lap top with you?" I asked ignoring his question. "See what you can find out about the tag number on the car at Marrie's and see what you can find out from the driver's licenses of the two creeps in the desert. Did you find any names of interest while you were in Canada?"

"I found out about bankers, insurance agents, and property managers and that there's a whole lot of money involved. Nothing gave me any leads as to Esaugetuh's whereabouts. About that list of names? I was wondering if you've considered reversing it. It seems to me that whoever is out to get you believe you're following the names as they appear on the list."

"Man, you just might be right! Let's begin at the bottom and then pop to the middle. That might buy us some time. While you're doing the computer search, I want to go over Esaugetuh's letter once again. Do you still have the letter he sent you and if you do may I see it?"

"Sure. No problem. It's right there in my backpack."

"That's it! That's how they knew where we were and what we were doing," I said holding up Esaugetuh's letter.

"What?

"The credit card. Esaugetuh gave you a credit card to use while you tracked me down. Someone has access to that account."

"How does that account for finding you in Reno? I wasn't with you," Running-water said.

"Hmm, you're right. But can you find out who accessed that account and on what dates? I asked.

"I can find out how many times and when but not sure about finding out by whom."

"Good!

I went to bed while Running-water continued working at his computer. I don't know what time it was when he packed it in. Around three a.m. I suddenly sat straight up in bed. Every neuron in my body was firing simultaneously. There was a sense of terrible danger all around me. I grabbed my gun and turned on the light.

Running-water, still in his street clothes, was asleep on his bed. Shaking him, I motioned for him to be very quiet. Seeing I had my gun, he pulled his from under his pillow.

"Smell it? Gasoline," I said.

"Yeah. Want to bet the door is jammed?"

Just in case someone was listening at the door, Running-water went into the bathroom, flushed the toilet, then doused the lights, and then tried the door. It was jammed.

The window, one of those that didn't open, shattered as he threw a table through it. Rapid fire of an automatic greeted that action. We both hit the floor and bullets continued to whiz over our heads.

"The mirror. I'll get it. It'll let us see out there." Running-water said as he bellied across the floor. As he did, he tossed me the duffle containing the money.

More shots, random rapid firing. The smell of gasoline permeated the room. Whoever it was must have poured it under the door. With some effort, we angled the mirror so we could see the street. Nothing. Changing the angle slightly upward we caught the glimpse of something shinny on an electric power pole.

"You see what I see?" I whispered.

"Yeah. I can nail him from here."

"No. Both of us shoot the wires and transformer above him. That'll give us time to get out. He's trying to ignite the gas." I replied.

On the count of three, we both fired a complete round. Sparks were flying everywhere. The transformer exploded into flames. We jumped and hit the ground running. I still clutched the duffle and my gun as we hauled ass around the side of the building. We made it to the jeep just as there was another burst of gun fire and an explosion. Our room was a mass of flames.

"Well, there go our clothes, your computer, and the cell phone," I said. "At least we got out."

"Not to worry about the computer. I got everything right here on a flash drive. The cell phone's in your duffle. You got the money, we got wheels. Let's get the hell out of here."

"It's a hell of a note that Esaugetuh's will and letter are gone. That'll make matters more difficult." I said as we headed out of town and toward Flagstaff.

"Wrong again, good buddy. They're in the duffle. The only things we don't have are our clothes." Running-water smirked.

"What's so funny?"

"You in your sleep shorts, shirtless and shoeless. Can't you just imagine the looks we'll get if we check into a motel? Can't you just hear the talk? 'Looks like that big Brave has got himself a sweet young thing." Running-water was roaring with laughter.

"Watch your mouth," I said, laughing and gave him a cuff aside of his head.

While Running-water drove, I telephoned ahead to make sure the new pilot and navigator were on deck. I told them to meet us at the airport rather than at Marrie's. I snapped the phone shut and sat there thinking.

"Hey man, you're off somewhere. What's up?" Running-water said.

"I got this feeling that there might be something wrong with the plane."

"Call the airport security and have them check the plane."

"Be better if I ask for a bomb check. Damn. Whoever it is that wants me dead, sure has some connections. Maybe we better split up. No use you getting head blown off."

"Uh-uh. You're not getting rid of me. Besides, you need somebody to look out for your sorry ass."

It took a little doing but I finally convince the Flagstaff police department to send out the bomb squad and check the jet. My third call was to Marrie with a request for some clothes. It was midday by the time we got to Marrie's and hunger was gnawing at our guts. Not only did she have clothes to fit us, she also had a wonderful meat stew ready. We made short work of that.

Afterwards, she brought out a bottle I recognized as the kind of brandy Esaugetuh always served.

"Marrie, that bottle. Has Esaugetuh been here again?"

"Mercy no. He left it here way back when. Can't say that I remember but after what you two have been through I thought a drop might do you some good."

And it did. I felt safe and secure. Marrie wanted the details of the desert episode particularly the role of the snake. Satisfied she finally asked, "How do you see the snake?"

"What do you mean?" I replied.

"How do you see the snake—as friend or foe?"

"I have no opinion one way or another," I said.

"Well, you should. That snake saved your life. Do you have so much disdain for life that you cannot show some respect and gratitude?" Marrie was angry.

"Hold on, Marrie. Adam put water in his hand and gave it to that rattler." Running-water scolded. "It could have bitten him."

"I'm talking about his attitude, how he feels inside. Sure he gave the snake water but did he do it out of obligation or out of respect and gratitude for another living thing?"

"I have no recollection of any particular feelings at that time. I simply went to its aid. It was no big deal." I said as I tried to conceal my annoyance at this line of conversation.

"Adam, can water be separated from its wetness?" Marrie asked.

"Of course not."

"Then how can you separate your feelings from your actions? Each thing no matter how big or small should be viewed as a thing of worth and your feelings and actions should reflect that."

"Even when there are those who are trying to kill me? Come on! Be realistic. How in the hell can I respect them?" I was really steaming and probably would have said considerably more had my cell phone not vibrated.

The police department was reporting on their search of the Gulfstream; they had found a bomb, defused it, and now wanted to talk to me. I would meet them at the plane, rather than have them come to Marrie's.

"Marrie, tell your friends they can find their jeep at the airport, hanger seven," I said motioning to Running-water that we had to leave.

Running-water appointed himself as the official driver and that was okay with me. It gave me time to think. Marrie had upset me and the pain in my rib cage added to my general ill temper. Shit, I hadn't been disrespectful of that snake. The fact of the matter is, I was damn grateful. I don't see why I should have to bow down and kiss ass every time someone does something for me.

"You still don't get it do you?" came a voice.

"What was that you said?" I challenged Running-water.

"I didn't say anything. You okay?"

"Marrie was ticking me off. By the way, thanks for sticking up for me. I appreciate it."

"No problem."

When we arrived at the airport, we slowly wound our way past various terminals before we got to hanger seven. Along with the police, a hoard of media people surrounded the hanger.

"Damn. Just what we don't need," I said.

Running-water stopped the jeep.

We sat there, watching the paparazzi trying to get in closer to the plane. I was surprised the plane was still in the hanger. I thought it would have been moved out from the hanger and away from the terminal. Seemed to me it would have been safer than leaving it inside.

A police officer on a motorcycle pulled up alongside our jeep and told us to move on. Once he understood who we were and that we would not get out of the jeep until the news media was off the premises, he radioed ahead to the hanger. We also pointed out that the media people were on private property and there were No Trespassing signs posted. As soon as the press was out of the hanger Running-water drove the jeep to the opposite side and we entered through a side door and out of sight of prying cameras and microphones.

"You the one who called about a bomb?" said a man whose face seemed to be in a perpetual pout.

"I'm Adam and this is my associate, Running-water. Close the hanger."

"What? I guess you didn't hear my question, Mr. Adam?"

"I said close the hanger and I mean for it to be done now. The name is Adam, just Adam."

"Okay, okay. Close the friggin' doors."

As the huge doors began to close, two men made a dash for the opening.

"Stop them," ordered the pouter.

"Good. They might be the men hired to guard my plane and they may also have planted the bomb. Have you located my other pilot and the flight attendant?"

"According to the hotel, no one was registered there that fit your description."

"Did you send someone over there to check it out?" Running-water asked.

"Didn't see any reason."

"Might be a good idea," I said. "Where was the bomb located?"

"In the cockpit, a small device but it would have killed the pilot and navigator or incapacitated them so they couldn't fly the plane."

"How soon can my people board to check it out."

"As soon as we're finished. While that's going on, I'd like to ask you some questions. Why did you suspect your plane was rigged with a bomb?"

"I'll answer your questions." Running-water piped up. "I'm his attorney," he said as he led the officer to one side.

While Running-water occupied the detective, I talked with the new pilot and navigator; gave them our destination, told them to file a flight plan, and asked them to be armed. If they had problems with that, I'd replace them. Both being former SEALS, they had no objections. A barrage of loud voices at the side door stopped any further talk. It was Marrie's two friends. Running-water cleared it up and they came in. I wanted to pay them for the use of their jeep but they refused the money. I also asked them to get us several boxes of cartridges for our guns and bring them back to the hanger.

"Glad to Adam, but there's——." said the larger of the two men.

"One other thing," I said continuing my conversation with the pilot, "Get ground service in here to check the fuel, sump it yourself. Make sure it's up to standard, check for any contaminants particularly microorganisms. I don't want to get airborne and have problems. Go over everything, thoroughly. Overlook nothing. Even check the damn head. Glad to have you on the team."

When I turned to speak with Marrie's two friends, they were gone.

***

The setting sun began a symphony of colors so typical of Arizona–a chorus of brilliant oranges and gold with a copper gold playing base against the alto of the blue sky. Our surroundings bathed in afterglow added a nice warmth. The artist, by whatever name you want to call her, was putting on a three dimensional show unequaled anywhere on this blue sapphire we call earth. The pilot filed the flight plan and we were nearly ready to leave for an island in the Atlantic, the location of Dr. Christopher Saint-Michaels, the seventh name on our list. The night promised to be a good one for flying. Running-water and I had just enough time to buy some new clothes, pick up two more cell phones as well as a new lap top to replace the one lost in the motel fire. Marrie's two friends arrived with six boxes of ammo for each of us. They accepted payment this time and compensation for any damage to their jeep.

"Adam, there's something you—." the large man said.

"Got to get aboard. Thanks for the help." I said as Running-water and I boarded the jet.

Once airborne I looked over the information Running-water had found about Saint-Michaels on his computer. Saint-Michaels has a Ph.D. in physics as well as in mechanical engineering and nuclear medicine. He's the Director of the Institute of Light Sciences and Technologies. Very impressive. He has been doing research in futuristic technologies involving quantum computing and communication using light. One area especially caught my attention. Saint-Michaels was into psychokinesis.

Maybe that was how Esaugetuh got from place to place so quickly? Teleportation? Maybe that's the missing link. The people who are after me think I have the knowledge to teleport and they think it is something Esaugetuh gave me. It's not the money they're after. The excitement of this new revelation nearly put me into orbit. Running-water had gone to shower and I yelled for him to come quick. He did and I burst out laughing. The image was too much. Here was a guy over six feet tall, dripping wet, bare-ass naked, long black hair plastered to the sides of his head with a Forty-five in his hand.

"What's so damn funny? And why'd you yell for me to come out here? What's the matter?"

The laughter faded away and died in its own guilt as I focused on the man in front of me. I'd never really looked at him with or without clothes. He was just someone who was there, actually a non-being. All he asked of me was to be accepted, to be included. I felt ashamed because I had taken him for granted, ordered him around like a servant with absolutely no sense of appreciation for what he was.

"First you call me out here then you begin laughing like some damn drunken fool and now you're just staring at me like you've never seen a naked Indian before. Are you going to tell me what was so all damned important?

"I'm sorry, honest! It's just that you looked so damned funny, a wild man, sopping wet with a gun in your hand. Anyway, I think I know why I'm being pursued."

"This better be good."

After I finished my explanation, Running-water said, "That's just great. If you have the secret of this teleportation thing why have they tried to kill you instead of kidnapping you?"

With a knack I would learn to appreciate, Running-water had deflated my wonderful theory. This was the second time he had done that and I suspect it won't be the last.

"Damn! I was sure I had it figured out. Can you and that computer of yours find out who's financing Saint-Michaels? It might be helpful."

"No problem. You mind if I get some clothes on first?" He said turning to go back to the bedroom.

I gave him a catcall and he shot me a bird.

"By the way," I called after him, "Since when have you been a lawyer?"

"I do have a degree in law. And yes, I passed the bar exam."

His earlier computer searches revealed that the two men who died in the desert, as well as the two men in the car at Marrie's, were from Colorado. Even though I had been at Mesa Verde searching for Esaugetuh and met a lot of people there, I didn't recognize them or their names. They must have another connection. We had a surprise when it came to Saint-Michaels. The only backer of his research was Esaugetuh.

"I want to check something," Running-water said as he reached for the phone.

"Hold it! It might be bugged." I said.

"Well, having worked as a private detective, I know how to check that out," Running-water replied as he began to take the phone apart.

"Well," I said, "Is it bugged?"

"Yeah, right there it is. Gotcha. But I don't think it can be of any use from here."

"That's how they knew about Marrie's. You called me from the plane just before you landed."

"Damn. You're right. I should have checked it out."

"Who you calling?" I asked.

"My sister."

"Your sister? I didn't know you had a sister."

"Yeah, she works for the Bureau of Indian Affairs. Her Indian name is Laughing-water. Her Christian name is Daphne."

Seeing the puzzled look on my face, Running-water explained, "One of the men in the desert was a Native and I want to know what tribe he belonged to. She could find that out for us."

"How old is this sister of yours?" I asked.

"Ha! So you're normal after all. She's twenty-five and even if she's my sister I've got to admit she's one foxy chick."

"I had *you* figured for about twenty-five," I said.

"You're right on the button. She's my twin. As soon as I have this phone back together I can make that call."

A heavy thump on top of the plane causing it to shudder. There was a sudden acceleration and we shot straight up vertically. Everything in the cabin went flying by us. Rolling like tumbleweeds on an open prairie, we ended up at the back of the plane. Behind our plane, flares exploded and then the plane made a sharp roll to the left. We hung on the arms rests of the seats to prevent being tossed about. Just behind us, there was a massive explosion that turned the night into daylight. We felt the vibrations even as our plane raced to its max speed. Finally, we leveled and slowed to our normal cruising speed.

"Holy shit! What the hell happened?" Running-water said as he scrambled to his feet. Still clutching his gun, he headed toward the front of the plane.

"You guys okay back there?" The pilot said as he opened the cockpit door.

"What the hell's going on?" Running-water said.

"We had a visitor. Wanted to knock us down. We got 'em with the chaff. They tried to puncture the main cabin. By the way, why does your plane have a chaff box, to begin with?"

"What's a chaff box?" I asked.

"It's a box attached near the rear engine and is used to launch heat decoys, launch flares, and sometimes scientific instruments. The projectiles go out with the engines thrust; they get into its vortex and are primarily used to confuse missile attacks," the pilot said.

"I'm not sure why the plane has such a system. It has been on loan to a research institute. Perhaps the institute installed the system?" I said.

"Sorry about the mess but we had to knock him off before he had a second shot at us. We'll clean the cabin when we land and that'll be in about forty minutes. You wanted a chopper ready when we landed, right?"

"Right. Don't suppose you can fly one of those?" I asked.

"If it's got wings, motor or blades I can fly it. You have a location?"

"I can only tell you when it's spotted from the air."

"We have to file a flight plan." the pilot replied.

"Make it a tour of the island," Running-water said.

"No problem. Better get seated and fasten your belts."

CHAPTER 6 - CHRISTROPHER SAINT-MICHAELS

They shall lay hands on the sick, and they shall recover.
Mark v16:8

Once again, I had the plane put under tight security. Our pilot, Dutch, checked out the chopper, filed the flight plan and we were soon airborne. The navigator stayed with the plane during its inspection for damage. Heading due east, we flew along the edge of the emerald green island. The ocean was a cobalt jewel shimmering in the early morning sunlight and accented by the sparkle of a white sandy beach that seemed to stretch the full length of the island.

An old trawler plowed its way through the gently rolling water creating white foam as sea gulls hungrily followed looking for any sign of food tossed their way. The short flight brought us over a large compound situated at the tip of a high cliff.

We circled the estate and made note that there were no visible access roads leading to or from its grounds. A closer look revealed a massive reproduction of Jefferson's Monticello from the pillars to the dome to outbuildings it was an exact copy. We also noted there wasn't a pad for us to land on and as we buzzed the place, no one seemed to be about the grounds or at the windows as we hovered outside trying to look in.

Dutch took the chopper back out over the water and did a 180 degree turn and brought us back in, setting us down on the beach as close to the cliff as possible. As soon as we hit the ground, two men, brandishing an Uzi, greeted us. Each had side arms and a grenade belt.

"Yer on private property. Take off!" said a burly man.

"Tell Saint-Michaels Adam's here," Running-water said.

The two men looked at one another. The burly one whipped out a phone, turned his back to us, and spoke to someone. When he had finished he turned and said, "You can't leave the chopper here. Wheel it inside and then follow me."

A large portion of the cliff began to move and once fully open it revealed a hanger. One of the men told us to line the chopper up with some rails that came up out of the sand. I noted that these rails lead from the hanger directly into the water. Inside were two helicopters, a high speed cigarette boat, and a jeep. I thought that was odd since there weren't any roads to or from the estate. The three of us followed the two men to a glass elevator.

Within seconds, we were looking into a huge open area containing pedestaled busts of the great philosophers and scientists from ancient times to modern including one of Stephen Hawking. Each had a plaque and each had its own spotlight. A huge spiral staircase seemingly suspended in mid-air led to an upper balcony that circled the dome. The glass steps held in place with golden colored chains did not sway. There didn't appear to be any rooms leading from the balcony.

"We're moving," Running-water whispered. "The whole room is moving."

"What is it you want?" The voice came from a figure standing at the top of the spiral stairs. It was a strange sight. The figure, bathed in an amber radiance, slowly descended the stairs.

"It's a hologram," Running-water said.

"I think the question is what may I do for you, Dr. Saint-Michaels? Perhaps a cut in your funding would be in order," I said. The hologram died. It was so quiet I could hear my own heart beating. A panel in the wall opened and in walked a tall stately man with silver hair. I would guess he was in his sixties. His clothes from head to toe spoke of money. Even his glasses evoked a sense of one accustomed to wealth.

"I'm Christopher Saint-Michaels. What is it you want?"

There was no detectable accent or regional dialect in his voice. It was non-expressive. I noticed he wore a large ring on his right hand. Its stone was blood-red with a yin/yang symbol set in gold. His left hand's index finger maintained a nervous twitch.

"I'm Adam. Your name was on a list I got from Esaugetuh."

"Ah! Esaugetuh. Yes, of course. Please forgive me. I didn't make the connection. You are his son. Please come with me. We don't get many visitors and they are not encouraged because of the work that goes on here."

We left through yet another passageway and came out onto a terrace overlooking the ocean. The view was breathtaking. Waves gently washed the sandy beach leaving ephemeral mosaics as they receded. A table had been set with linen, expensive china, and silver. A large fruit compote of crystal and silver sat in the middle of the table. It contained a variety of fresh tropical fruits. Smaller silver dishes containing small squares of bread and different kinds of cheese evenly placed around the compote. Saint-Michaels indicated we should take a seat.

Impressive, I thought. Guess we were expected, after all.

A handsome Indonesian man came out and offered us brandy, which he poured from a cut crystal decanter into snifters. While this was going on, I wondered if such opulence was essential for quality scientific research. Was this what Esaugetuh's money was being used for?

"At the risk of seeming to be rude, I must ask again what it is you want."

"And as Adam said, the question is what can he do for you? I believe your grant is up for renewal. And as such I would think a firsthand progress report on your research would be in order," Running-water said.

Saint-Michaels' demeanor immediately changed from polite tolerance to near hostility.

"My contract does not require a progress report. I don't have time for such nonsense."

"Adam, I don't think you should continue any further support of the research going on here. The twenty-five million that has been invested is quite enough," Running-water said.

"I have questions about Esaugetuh I want to ask Dr. Saint-Michaels if he doesn't mind."

"Ah, yes! Esaugetuh. Be brief. I don't have time for such things."

"When was the last time you had direct contact with him?"

"Direct contact? Hmm. It's been at least a couple of years, maybe longer.

"At that time did he indicate what he was doing or planning to do?"

"Well, he mentioned you. Said he had adopted you. I didn't realize that you were an adult. Very unusual for someone to adopt an adult."

"Has he visited your Institute before?"

"No. We met in Denver at a symposium."

"Have you received any written communication from him since then?"

"You mean besides the yearly check?"

"Yes. I'm trying to find out what he did during the past two years."

"Why don't you just ask him?"

"He's disappeared."

"I don't understand. I got my yearly check from him just last week."

"Was it signed?"

"Come to think of it, no. It's one of those bank checks. I did get a letter from him sometime back and I may still have it. You're welcome to it."

Saint-Michaels pushed a button on his Android. Spoke to someone.

"The letter will be brought to you."

"I'd appreciate that. Thank you."

A woman in her mid-forties came out onto the terrace and handed Saint-Michaels an envelope that he in turn handed to me.

"Tell me, do you know of any reason anyone would want me dead?" I said as I opened the letter.

My question caught Saint-Michaels totally off guard.

"No—no I don't. Someone has tried to kill you.

"Yes."

"Good god! Why?"

"That's what we'd like to know," Running-water said.

"Is that letter any help?"

"He mentions a person named Nick Sears. Do you know who that is and what his connection to Esaugetuh might be?"

"That's the third time that same old trawler has gone by. It looks like the one we flew over on our way in." Running-water said.

"Hmm. Might be a good idea to check it out. Have you binoculars to check it out?" I asked.

"Something better," Saint-Michaels said as he opened a small case containing a computer. Evidently, he had it with him when we came out to the terrace and I simply had not noticed it.

He folded back the linen tablecloth and there soon appeared a clear image of the old ship. With magnification, we could see a rocket launcher being readied. Saint-Michaels continued to work the keyboard of the computer. We heard a whirring noise and within a picosecond, the image on the monitor exploded. We looked out to sea and the ship was ablaze. The cigarette boat that I had seen when we arrived was speeding toward the burning ship. It contained two men.

"Listen," Saint-Michaels said.

"There are at least six people in the water. Should we pick them up, sir?"

"No. Give them flotation and then board the ship. Sweep it," Saint-Michaels said.

"How the hell did you pull that off?" Running-water said.

"Laser. It's very effective for relatively short distances. Good thing you noticed that trawler."

"Sir. We've found four more on board. The sweep of the ship has been completed. What do you want me to do with these men?"

"Bring them here and sink the ship. We'll meet you in the lower chamber. Come with me."

I counted nine floors as we descended down into the interior of the cliff. As we made the descent, I told Saint-Michaels of the plane incident. This seemed to confuse him. It was difficult to read him, to know what he was thinking. It was not clear in my own mind if he was friend or foe.

The speed boat soon arrived with the men from the trawler, four inside, and six on the flotation device behind the boat.

"Keep your friggin' legs spread or I'll cut your balls off," the burly man said, as he searched each man.

He's enjoying giving those men pain, I thought as I glanced over at Running-water. I noticed Dutch had his fists clinched.

Finally, the burly man completed his search of each of the ten men. It was fortunate for them that none had any concealed weapons because I'm sure he would have inflicted even worse pain and enjoyed doing it.

After an hour of interrogation by Saint-Michaels, we weren't any closer to answers than we were when he began. It seemed to me that this wasn't the first incident of this nature to have confronted Saint-Michaels.

The burly man interrupted the questioning and handed Saint-Michaels several bags of stuff from the burning ship. Saint-Michaels immediately emptied each onto the floor. He appeared to be searching for something very specific.

"What are you looking for? Perhaps I can help." I said.

"What? Oh. Nothing in particular, just looking."

"Mind if I take a look?"

"I don't see anything of interest, but go ahead."

My search brought forth a small notebook. I concealed it from Saint-Michaels by using one of the sleight of hand tricks I learned from Esaugetuh. As soon as I had palmed it off to Running-water, I asked if I might talk with one of the trawler's crew. No objection being raised, I chose the one man who had been ignored and who seemed to hang back a bit. His eyes told me he was more than a deck hand and as the others, he had played dumb and gave vacuous answers to questions.

"I'd like to talk to this man alone. Could you remove the others?"

"Of course," Saint-Michaels said as he gestured for them to be removed.

Once the other men were removed from the immediate area, I turned to the remaining man. For a time I did nothing but look at him, gradually forcing his eyes to meet mine.

He looked directly at me and I locked his gaze. I then placed one finger on the bridge of his nose and moved it ever so slowly down to his lips. There was an abject terror in his whole being. Every nerve in his body was screaming. Wetness began to show on the front of his pants and it grew in size until they were soaking wet. He began to tremble and his shaking became so violent that he collapsed, whimpering like a small child who had been scolded.

Kneeling down to him and cupping his face in my hands, I gently wiped his tears away with my thumbs.

"Will you talk to me?"

"Y-y-yes. I–."

"Good. Why did you try to blow up this place?"

"Hired to do it. We're testing a new short range missile."

"Against an occupied dwelling? Didn't that seem strange to you?"

"We were told it was empty and was going to be demolished."

"Who told you all of this?"

"I don't know his name. He just called and the stuff was delivered to my ship."

"Where'd he call from? Do you have any idea as to who this man might be?"

"No. Wait! The ship's radio system always recorded calls. You can get it from the ship."

"The ship's been sunk."

"True, but the radio room wasn't hit."

"How many rockets did you have on board?"

"Three."

"Where's your ship registered?"

"Haiti."

I held his head in my hands once more. I felt the muscles of his face tighten and the rapid fire of his synapses.

"Relax. I am not going to hurt you. No one is going to hurt you. Feel the warmth. Let it flow through your whole body. Breathe slowly. When you feel comfortable, I have one more question. If you were paid to do this, where's the money?"

"It was in my cabin."

"Thank you," I said as I released him.

"How did you get him to talk and how did you know he was the captain?" Saint-Michaels said.

"Can you get the recorder from the ship?"

"Yes. Strange about the money, don't you think?"

"There's one more bag that your man didn't empty. It's over there on the other side of the boat. Give it to the captain and set him and his crew free."

"Mister." said the captain. "There is something else."

"Yes. I know. Do you want to tell me about it now?" I said.

"I never meant to hurt anybody. I didn't know you were here until I saw you on the deck. I called the man. He wanted me to give him a description of the people on the deck. When I described you to him, he got excited and ordered me to launch the rocket immediately. He was screaming at me. I didn't know what to do. My crew needed the money. I needed the money for my family. Please, please! You've got to understand."

"You remember the number?"

"Yes."

"Call."

I handed him a cell phone.

There was no answer. Running-water said he could use his computer and the number to get a name, an address, and even a map. While he was doing that I took

Saint-Michaels aside and again emphasized that the ship's captain and his crew were to be set free with all of the money. My pilot would take them back to the city. He'd have to make a couple of trips. Saint-Michaels agreed and he caught the implication that his men may not be as trustworthy as he thought.

Soon the captain and his men were on their way. On our way back to the top, Saint-Michaels said, "I'd be honored if you would stay over and join me for dinner."

"Thanks. Perhaps then, we can get a better understanding about your research," I said.

I had no intention of letting him off the hook.

During the meal of wonderfully prepared seafood, I noticed that Saint-Michaels had paled and that his complexion had become ashen gray.

"Christopher," I said, "Lay down on the floor immediately."

"What?" Running-water said.

"Help me get him on the floor. He's having a heart attack."

We loosened his clothing, opened his coat and shirt to help him breathe easier. Panic seized him as he fought to remain conscious.

"Make sure no one comes in here," I said to Running-water.

I moved my hands over his chest and I felt the life force draining from his body. With both hands firmly on his chest, I slowly applied pressure. The heat of my hands began to transfer to his chest, his energetic matrix steadied and gradually began to strengthen. The gurgle in his heart's lower chamber stopped. His eyes fluttered and his breathing steadied.

My hands were burning up. The skin cracked and small trickles of blood dried as soon as they surfaced. I cried out in pain and that brought Running-water to my side.

"My god! Your hands are hemorrhaging," he said as he grabbed a glass of water from our dinner table and poured it over my hands. Then, he gently wrapped both in cloth napkins.

"Help me get Christopher inside. We need to get him to a hospital."

The burly man and the Indonesian appeared.

"Get your chopper ready. Fly Dr. Saint-Michaels to the airport. My plane will fly him to the mainland. He needs medical attention right away," I said.

"Well, what's wrong with him? He seems okay to me."

'Listen you asshole, do as Adam says or I'll blow your head off," Running-water said.

Upon my insistence, Running-water went with them to the airport. As they lifted off, I called the plane and told Dutch to prepare to take Saint-Michaels to the mainland.

With them gone, I took the opportunity to check out my surroundings. Beneath the main house, down inside the cliff, there were several rooms. Most were locked, however; the one I accessed contained surveillance monitors showing those rooms to which I could not gain entrance. These were filled with an array of scientific equipment.

During my camera tour, I only saw one other human being, the Indonesian who was in his own chambers. The rooms that Running-water and I were assigned were also monitored. One screen was blank and it remained that way no matter what I did. Even the air space surrounding the estate, the ocean and its beach were shown. I noticed a small object coming toward the compound. It was the helicopter returning. I went down to the beach.

The rotor blades had barely stopped when Running-water dragged the burly man out of the chopper and jumped on him. His fists were flying so fast I could barely see them.

"For god's sake don't just stand there. Get this maniac off me."

"Shut your frigging mouth you scum bag. Shut up or I'll cut you bad." Running-water said as he whipped out a sticker.

I grabbed Running-water by his long braid and yanked his head back, catching him under his chin with my other hand. He fell backwards and the burly man rolled and sprang to his feet. He lunged for Running-water but met the flat of my hand in his face. His neck snapped and he fell to the ground. Running-water was squatted, Indian style, and ready to gut with his knife.

Stepping in front of him, I held out my hand, palm up, and said, "What the hell is wrong with you?"

"That son of -a-bitch tried to push me out of the chopper. Said he'd finish you when he landed. He's pissed because you found out he had the money and made Saint-Michaels give it to the captain and his crew."

"Man, you sure were steamed," I said.

"Is the bastard dead?"

"No, but he does have a broken neck. There must be a first aid kit around here somewhere. Get me some bandages and make some splints. We will need to stabilize him before moving him. "

"May I help?" It was the Indonesian.

"Don't suppose you have a stretcher, do you? By the way, do you have a name?"

"Yes to both of your questions. My name is Kim Su. I'll bring you a stretcher. May I ask a question, Mr. Adam?"

"Fire away."

"Why do you help this man? He is a bad man."

"He is of value."

"Ah, you will torture him to make him talk," Kim Su said.

"No, no! He has value because he is. He exists."

"I don't understand."

"Each living thing has its own value and worth because it is unique unto itself. We respect that. It troubles me that I had to use force to stop further violence but sometimes such force is necessary for the preservation of the good."

"You are too much."

"No, just Adam."

"Mr. Adam, I have another question. What is this good you mention?"

"Ah! Philosophers have argued that one since the beginning of time. For me, it means that each existent thing has a right to exist, and should be granted respect because of that existence."

"But what if that person murders?"

"Violent acts committed against innocent people are inexcusable and should be viewed as an abhorrence but the persons who commit those types of acts still deserve to be viewed as human beings not for what they have done but because they are—they exist! To do otherwise lowers you to the same level of unacceptable behavior. We make judgment about the action. A very wise man once said that if you really get involved in examining those qualities that make a person unique you will forget about judging him; you may not come to love him but you will cease hating him."

I paused.

"There. Those splints should hold. Help me slide the stretcher beneath him."

Once we got the burly man into the hanger, the three of us got the helicopter on to the tracks. Kim Su brought it on in. Running-water was in a pout because I had interfered.

"Kim Su, does this guy have a name?" I asked.

"Yes. His name is Aloysius Samuel Simpson. Ass for short." Kim Su said with gleeful vengeance.

Running-water and I both burst out laughing. The name was so out of sync with what we had observed.

"How about Al?" I said.

We carefully put Al on the elevator and whisked him up to the main floor. Kim Su showed us Al's quarters and we rolled him into bed. My cell phone rang. It was Dutch. I was glad to hear Saint-Michaels was resting comfortably. I asked him to get a collar for a person with a broken neck.

"Why didn't you let him kill me?" Al said.

"Your death would have solved nothing. Why did you try to kill Running-water?"

"Because you two were responsible for me having to give up all that money."

"But surely Saint-Michaels pays you very well," I said.

"I want to get off this stinking island. It's driving me nuts. If I leave, I have no income. That money would have set me up for life."

"I'll speak to Saint-Michaels and see if he won't set up a modest annuity for you and help you find other employment on the mainland. Surely you were allowed out of the compound and could go anywhere on the island you wanted. You must have friends, acquaintances, or a lady?"

"Women. Sure. Plenty. After a while they're all the same. Friends? None that you would trust with your back to them. Man, you're the lucky one. You got that Running-water."

Looking at Running-water, I noticed an obvious coloring in his cheeks.

"What?"

"Nothing."

"Al, isn't the real problem your lack of trust? You don't trust anyone and you don't believe that any woman would want just you, would want to build something of value together with you."

"Look," Al said, "I'm sorry about all of this. I really am. You have to understand that Saint-Michaels is sort of weird. After a while, it gets to you. I hear him talking and there's no one there. Sometimes he forgets things; he even forgets what day it is. He's so wrapped up in whatever it is he's doing. You were looking for a friend. I think he was here. I heard Saint-Michaels talking to someone he called Esaugetuh."

"I'm sure you are sorry. We'll not discuss this incident again. Right now, you need to rest. As soon as the neck brace gets here, I'll put that on you."

"We need to really make a search of this place. Saint-Michaels probably has Esaugetuh locked up here somewhere, a prisoner." Running-water said.

"I find it unusual that there aren't other people around here. For example, housekeepers, cooks, or grounds people?"

"Yeah, and where's the woman who brought you Esaugetuh's letter? Let's go."

As we left Al's quarters, he said, "There's a central monitoring system below ground."

"Thanks. We'll begin there, " I said, not bothering to tell him I had already been there.

Within seconds, we were below ground.

Running-water accessed the system and got the monitors I couldn't get to work, turned on. On one, we could see the kitchen, large and ultramodern with wine cellar, pantries, and a small alcove containing a chair and couch.

We next located several other smaller quarters that consisted of a bath, bedroom, and sitting room. Each contained a television and an intercom. With some adept keyboarding, Running-water brought into view Saint-Michaels private quarters? It was a spacious area with a view of the ocean and as with the other living quarters, it contained a sitting room. Large brown leather chairs, desk, and wall to wall and floor to ceiling bookcases filled the space. Another anteroom contained two high-backed leather chairs, a marble table with a single figurine lamp crowned with a dark green shade. A cabinet along one wall seemed out of place until I realized it was a humidor for cigars. The room was for smoking. Yet I did not detect any cigar odor on Saint-Michaels. After examining five separate quarters, the master suite, kitchen, and the main public room we still had not found anything unusual.

"You know what?" Running-water asked. "We haven't seen any people in these other rooms."

"Hmm. Strange. Wonder why? Is it possible we are watching a video on these monitors?

"Let's find out. I'll just pull this fire alarm." Running-water said.

Within minutes of the clanging alarm, we followed five people as they left the building.

"Well that answers the question about watching a video," I said.

Like two voyeurs, we watched a mini drama unfold in Al's quarters.

Unable to get up because I had strapped him down so he wouldn't do more damage to his neck, he began hollering for help. His door flew open and in rushed the woman who brought me the letter.

"Everything is going to be okay. Not to worry. I'll get you out," she said.

She rolled him over onto her own back. Even though there was no smoke, she slowly crawled out of his rooms. Glued to the monitors we watched as she struggled to get down a long interior corridor and exit.

Running-water punched another button on the console and brought up a view of the grounds. There, we watched the woman gently she roll Al on to the ground and help him get up. She tore a piece from her dress and wiped his brow.

"Well, I'll be damned. She's in love with him. And he's so dumb he doesn't even know it." I said.

"What are you talking about?"

"Nothing. I count seven people. How about you?"

"Yeah, seven. Now what?"

"Shut off the alarm for one thing. There must be a way to communicate with all of them at once. Each of their living quarters has an intercom."

"No problem. Speak" Running-water said as he handed me a mike.

"Please assemble in the public room. There is no fire. I repeat, there is no fire."

One by one seven people filed into the rotunda. Confused, they huddled together, unsure of what was going to happen.

By now, they had heard of the attack by the ship, the collapse of Dr. Saint-Michaels, and the fight with Al. They quieted as Running-water and I stepped into the room.

"I am Adam and I want to explain to you what happened to Dr. Saint-Michaels. He's suffered a heart attack and I had him flown to the mainland for examination and treatment. The latest information I have is that he is resting comfortably. Al, here, has a broken neck and will be in a brace as soon as it arrives. Because we didn't know how many of you there were, it was necessary to pull the fire alarm. For that, I apologize."

"When will you know more about the doctor?" said the woman.

"What is your name? " I asked.

"I'm called Odora."

"Well, Odora, I hope to hear very soon. That was a very brave thing you did for Al."

"What do you mean?"

"Carrying him out on your back as you crawled on your hands and knees. You must think a great deal of him."

Her face turned rose red and she looked away. However, it didn't go unnoticed. Al reached up and touched her hand.

Perhaps there's room for love, after all, I thought.

My cell phone rang. Saint-Michaels was okay and upon his insistence was on his way back to the island. I told the seven people in the rotunda the news about Saint Michaels. The relief shown on their faces told me a great deal about Saint-Michaels but not enough to erase the uneasiness I felt.

"How does a starving man get something to eat around here?" Running-water said.

"I will bring you some hot food right away," Odora said. "Mr. Adam, will you take food also?"

"Yes. And, Odora, could you prepare something suitable for Dr. Saint-Michaels? He'll be here in a couple of hours."

"Would you have a brandy before your food or after?" Kim Su said.

"We would like all of you to join us. Kim Su, I think it would be appropriate to serve everyone a brandy before all of us sit down to eat."

"Meet on the terrace and from there we can watch for Dr. Saint-Michaels," Running-water said.

The brandy relaxed them enough so they felt more talkative. It seems they have a great deal of respect for Saint-Michaels, but find him cold and almost unfriendly. We learned that Saint-Michaels had one rule that he insisted absolute obedience to. No one pries into his work.

Hmm. Maybe that's why he bristled when Runningwater asked for a progress report, I thought.

Odora served up a wonderful buffet of shrimp, various cuts of meats, cheeses, and fresh fruit.

While we ate, we watched the moon make her journey up out of the sea. She was so beautiful, her size dwarfing the evening sky while her brightness paled the stars. Moon glow showered each of us in a subtle silver yellow creating a gentler and kinder bondage. Odora was supplicant in her attentiveness to Al.

Sweet jasmine and star honeysuckle perfumed the air as sea breezes floated up from below. The swoosh of the waves against the cliff announced the arrival of the tide. As their sounds sunk into my consciousness I realized that Dutch would not be able to land on the beach.

"Where is the chopper to land? The tide is coming in." I asked.

"Not to worry, Mr. Adam. The doctor will tell your man where to land." Kim Su said.

"I hear it. The helicopter. It's coming." Odora said.

Its lights soon came into view. As it whizzed over the top of the house its search lights came on. Then silence. Noting my concern Kim Su informed me there was a landing pad that was also an elevator. It had the chopper down to the hanger before its blades stopped rotating.

Shortly Dutch and Saint-Michaels made their entrance.

"I don't need a wheel chair. I don't care what the doctor said."

"Stay," Dutch said.

"Adam"

"Dr. Saint-Michaels," I said.

"You're quite something, young man. By all accounts, including my own, I should be quite dead.

Generally, when the heart over fills with blood, it ruptures. You are a very powerful man. Esaugetuh said you would be very powerful."

"I'm not so sure about that."

"What happened to him?" Saint-Michaels said looking at Al.

"He has a broken neck."

"You didn't heal him?"

"Not completely. Apparently, my energies have to rebuild and since I really depleted them on you I wasn't able to help Al very much."

"Nice job with the brace. We'll get the other one on as soon as I take an x-ray. Take him down to the medical lab."

"Yes sir," said Kim Su.

"What's wrong with your hands, Adam? You better come down to the med lab also. Let me take a look at them."

"Not so fast Dr. Saint-Michaels. The doctors ordered you to bed and that's where you are going— to bed," Dutch said.

"You must rest. Al and I will be just fine. You can check us over in the morning. If you don't rest and your heart acts up again I may not be able to help you."

"On condition, you tell me about your healing powers."

"On condition, you answer my questions?" I replied.

"Very well. If you need anything just ask Mr. Kim Su."

In our quarters, we located and disconnected the camera and mike. Running-water removed the bloodied bandages from my hands. They were swollen and painful, another new experience. Whatever the physical transformation going on in my body it was surely an arresting experience.

"Thanks, Adam," Running-water said.

"For what?" I said.

"For pulling me off Al. I would have killed him, you know."

"Yes, I know. And we would have lost a good deal of information and more importantly a potential ally and I would have lost a friend."

"Well, just what would you have done if that bastard was trying to push you out of the damn chopper?"

"I probably would have killed him. Then I would have died also."

"How so?"

"I can't fly a helicopter. Can you?" I said laughing.

"Hell no."

It was now customary for one of us to stand guard while the other slept. I won the toss and took the first watch. Actually, I was grateful for some quiet time. The view from our window showed an army of stars and moon glow reflected on the water.

Tapping at our window brought me to full attention. An outline of a large figure filled the frame. My gun was at the ready. The window opened.

"Saint-Michaels is talking to your missing friend."

It was Al.

"Are you sure?" I whispered.

"Yes. Come."

I started for our bedroom door but Al motioned for me to follow him through the open window. There was a very small balcony with a door leading into the house. A dimly lighted passage way led to a narrow set of stairs. These we followed until we arrived at another hallway. Al slowly pushed open a sliding door just enough for me to see Saint-Michaels standing with his back to us. He was talking to someone just out of my view.

I immediately recognized the voice as that of Esaugetuh. Before Al could stop me, I was into the room. My sudden intrusion threw Saint-Michaels totally off guard. Much to my surprise, there was no one else in the room.

"Where is he?" I growled.

"How dare you come in here? Get out. You've ruined everything."

"I dare whatever I damn well, please. Answer my question and do it now."

"I have nothing to say to you. I want you out of here by morning. And you," he said turning to Al, "You are fired."

"Stay right where you are Al. The fireworks are about to begin."

The room had a waffle-domed ceiling that would make a great resonator for an energy burst. For quite some time, I had been practicing giving off small bursts of energy from one hand to the other. Depending on the atmospheric conditions, I could actually make an electrical arc from my hands to another object. I wasn't even sure it would work in here but it was worth a try if it got Saint-Michaels to talk.

I walked around him seven times; each time I raised my right hand toward the domed ceiling and each time I drew the circle closer to the outer wall. By that time, I figured I had built up enough static electricity to create an arc. I touched a metal electrical covering. The lights flickered, went out, and then it began: An electrical dance of blue-white twirling around the inner circle of the dome, arcing from my outstretched hand, and gathering momentum, flashing down the sides of the room, across the floor and stopping at Saint-Michaels' feet. He screamed and collapsed.

"My god, what are you?" Al gasped.

Saint-Michaels lay cowering in a heap on the floor. But before I could answer Al, Running-water kicked in the sliding door, with a gun in each hand, demanded to know what was going on. Al immediately put his hands, folded, behind his head.

"Please, please no more. What do you want to know?" Saint-Michaels said. "I should have known that when Esaugetuh said you were very powerful that he meant it."

"Good. Begin with this room and where Esaugetuh went." I said.

"Esaugetuh is not here. He has never been here."

"I heard his voice."

"You heard recordings made months and months ago. This room is is a sound receptor. While we were at the Denver symposium Esaugetuh was kind enough to participate in a telepathic communications experiment. He would project his thoughts and I would receive them as voice communication. I would then notify him that I had or had not received his messages. I recorded those messages. Suddenly, there was no more communication from him. I have been playing them over and over again to see if I could determine what the source of the problem is."

"Why didn't you just call him? You said you notified him that you received his voice," Running-water said.

"I simply left a message on a recorder. There was no other communication."

"How do you know that the voices you have recorded are Esaugetuh's?" I said.

"We had an agreed upon code."

"Which is?" Running-water said.

"Adam. Each message would contain information about Adam."

"Hmm. It might be a good idea if we listened to all of these recordings," I said.

Saint-Michaels composed himself and agreed to play all of the recordings. Each one revealed something about a person called Adam, his physical appearance, his innate powers, and his ability to heal. He spoke of Adam as an adopted son. The rest of the messages dealt with mundane items such as the time of day, the weather, and sometimes he would mention the date. It was Running-water and his legal mind-set that discovered an important piece of information.

He poked me.

"What?"

"These recordings were made before you met up with Esaugetuh."

The dates had not registered with me. I shuddered at the implications and that didn't go unnoticed.

"You okay, Adam?" Running-water said.

"Fine. No problem. Dr. Saint-Michaels do you think it is possible for Esaugetuh to communicate directly with me via telepathic means?"

"I suppose so. Have you had such an experience?"

"Yes. Several times. I hear a voice, not quite the usual voice I recognize as Esaugetuh's but nonetheless, his voice. It seems to come out of nowhere."

"Have you had this experience recently?" Saint-Michaels said.

"Yes."

"Hmm! Are you willing to participate in a little experiment?"

"Sure."

"This resonating chamber is made of semiconducting materials with an ultra-thin cap or micro disk. Ultrasound speakers are embedded in the waffled interior ceiling structure while the sides are deliberately smooth. Involved here are the principles used in frequency-doubling within nonlinear optical crystals. What I've attempted to do is to get the frequencies close enough so that they can become audible, that is, so they can be heard in this chamber. I designed it to pick up the slightest directed sound and magnify it to an audible level. If we assume that Esaugetuh is still attempting thought-projection then somewhere along the line there exists a problem. My system is constructed to receive only from a specified source. In this case, that is Esaugetuh. Because the chamber is anechoic, it is echo free and free from other disturbing sounds such as jet planes or the chatter of birds. However, I have found it is quite sensitive to humidity and the extra body heat may have a negative effect. Your friend will have to leave and that other person is to get off my property immediately."

"First of all doc, I'm not leaving. Wherever Adam is I am

also. You got that?" Running-water said.

"You're sure sounding mighty biblical," I said to Running-water. "Al is to remain. Perhaps if you took the time to know the people who work for you, you would find them really a great group. They each have names, and faces that go with those names, each has a set of feelings, and each has dreams and hopes. Above all, they have the right to be treated with dignity and respect."

"I don't need to be lectured by you, young man. In fact, I've had enough of you and your henchmen. I want all of you out of here and off my property now," Saint-Michaels said.

"You still don't get it, do you, doc? You don't own this property, the equipment in the labs, the planes, and boat, or even the house furnishings. The Institute does. It owns everything and Adam here is the Institute. If anyone gets out it will be you," Running-water said, stepping closer to Saint-Michaels.

"You can't bluff me. I've owned this property for over thirty years."

"Wrong! The title to this property and all its contents were transferred to the Institute last year, that is, to Adam. Perhaps if you read your mail you would have understood that. Your personal stake was revoked and you became an employee. You agreed to that when you signed the last check sent to you," Running-water said.

"How do you know all of this?" I said, shaking my head in amazement.

"You'd be surprised what you can find out using a computer. Your charade is over, doc."

"How dare you call my work a charade? I've made significant progress. Researchers have brought light to a dead stop. [6] Their research is significant to my work in using light in quantum communication. Eventually, it will be important to psychokinesis," Saint-Michaels said.

"Your labs are filled with fake equipment built for Hollywood science fiction movies. That's why you allowed no one to enter the labs. Even a child would know they were fake," Running-water said.

Again I asked, "How do you know all of this?"

"You are not the only one who prowls around at night. When we viewed the individual rooms on the monitors in the control room, I noticed there wasn't any fancy security at the doors. There were just ordinary doors with ordinary locks. I picked the locks."

"And Esaugetuh's voice in the resonating chamber?"

"Just a recording. The room, like the other labs, is a fake. Probably it would have worked had it been connected to a listening device like those used in SETI [7]. As it is, I don't think it's any more than a lightning catcher."

"No wonder my energy charge gave such a display."

"Right. All that wiring magnified it. Wonder you didn't get us all killed."

"That still leaves us with the question of why Saint-Michaels is on my list," I said.

"Maybe he wasn't the one you were to deal with."

"Okay, if not him, who then?"

"I don't know. But I think we are finished here."

"Wait! This dome is a listening dish. I told you I had recorded Esaugetuh's messages and you listened to them. You recognized his voice. He said things about you that only he would know. The equipment your friend saw is not fake and I can prove it. You should at least give me the chance to substantiate my position. I am who I say I am," Saint-Michaels said.

"Let us assume that what you say is true but that does not explain your behavior toward us or your failure at being candid with us," I said.

"True. I have not been open. I have my reasons and they are good ones."

"Well, suppose you begin by telling us what they are," Running-water said.

"I was afraid you might steal my work and claim it as your own. You have to understand that there are those who would kill to have access to the work I have accomplished so far. Billions of dollars are at stake. Can you imagine being able to communicate at the speed of light? What that will do to communication technology, to the business world?"

"Why would you think that Adam would want to steal what is already his?" Running-water said.

"Well, I wasn't sure who you really were. I also saw you skulking around my compound. I have monitors in my chambers. That made me suspicious. And then I became very concerned that you would stop financing my work and everything would be lost."

"Okay, now what?" I said.

"Well, if you are still interested, we can attempt communication with Esaugetuh," Saint-Michaels said.

"Check Al's neck first. You said you had a med lab." I said.

"Very well. Let's see ah– your name is Al Simpson. Is that correct?"

"Yes, sir."

"Good. Come with me. You too Mr. Adam and Mr. Running-water."

The x-rays showed no damage to Al's neck. In fact, it was not necessary for him to keep the brace. He was one happy man. I had a distinct feeling that Odora would be very happy also. Maybe they are the real reason for my being here. Maybe Al had to see that he had value and thus could give value to someone else in the form of love. More importantly, maybe he had to realize that he was worthy enough to love.

"I want to thank you, Adam. You're really something. And Running-water, I'm sorry I tried to kill you. You're okay. No hard feelings, I hope," Al said as he extended his hand.

"No hard feelings," Running-water said.

"Let us go into the control room of the resonating chamber," [8] Dr. Saint-Michaels said.

Saint-Michaels opened a panel and began to make several adjustments of some kind. Noting my puzzlement, he explained that he was adjusting the skin of the microdish, turning on the power, programming the speakers, and checking the humidity and temperature.

"Can you go into a meditative state?" Saint-Michaels said.

"Yes. However, there is some preparation necessary. I need time to clear my mind and to get my total being balanced."

"Do it. Clear your mind of any thoughts. A thought is not unlike a being even though it has no size, weight, height, or length. It does have duration and because it does, it exerts enormous power. Behind thought is the whole force of nature and it is expressed in acts. You understand?"

"Yes," I replied.

"I want you to select a specific thought and when it has arrived on the physical level that is, when it is in a state of astral projection, I want you to release it. If Esaugetuh is out there and is receptive, it will be received and Esaugetuh's response or counterpart in the form of verbalization externalized."

"Whenever you are ready let me know," I said.

"Mr. Simpson and Mr. Running-water it would be best if you waited here in the control room. Four factors have an influence here: time, place, condition, and the human body. If everything is synchronized then a matrix will be formed through which a thought may be transposed into a verbalization that we can all hear."

I settled myself on the floor of the chamber, Indian fashion, and began a silent chant. Each repetition took my mind to another level of quietude. About fifteen minutes later, I felt sufficiently calmed to consider the message I would send to Esaugetuh. That determined I signaled Saint-Michaels that I was ready. The lights in the dome dimmed to a mere glow. I had selected a simple phrase, one that was common to me. I would think, but not verbalize, "I am Adam."

Saint-Michaels, Al, and Running-water were watching me via closed circuit television in the control room.

"Look at that. He's got a blue glow about him and it's changing to a gold color." Al said.

"I can't believe it. Just look at that halo surrounding his entire body! It's the color of the rainbow." Saint-Michaels said.

"You sure he's not in any danger in there?" Running-water said.

Saint-Michaels didn't have time to answer.

"And so you are!" boomed a voice that vibrated throughout the chamber.

An intense light flashed across one side of the chamber and then shot straight up causing the domed ceiling to glow a black purple. Saint-Michaels threw some switches, the lights came on, and Running-water rushed to Adam who sat fixated.

"Adam? You okay. Talk to me." Running-water said.

"Whew! That was something else. Did you hear it? The voice?" I said.

"Look! On the wall." Al said.

In bold letters burned deep into one wall of the chamber were the words:

Be as shifting sand.

If it was Esaugetuh's voice, where is he? What does the message on the wall mean? Is it from Esaugetuh or is it a trick by Saint-Michaels? Does Esaugetuh want me to continue tracking down the people on the list? Does he want me to keep looking for him? Does he know where I am? I am not sure at what point in time that I realized that my questions were now of a different nature; that a probing for answers to age old questions of humanity now seems to have changed to those that are very practical, very personal in terms of immediate survival. I wonder if this is to be the direction of my life now; survival questions, direct and immediate?

There was little time to continue being reflective. The alarms began screaming, "Intruder, Intruder" just like in the movies. Saint-Michaels yelled for us to get out of the chamber but it was too late. The lights went out and bullets were ricocheting everywhere. Then Running-water's twin Glock 10mms began nonstop return fire. Groans filled the air. More spurts from automatic weapons and then a single response.

Silence.

The acrid smell of spent shells was so strong it burned my throat. Inching my way along the wall I crawled toward the control room. I bumped into a body. It didn't move so I crawled on. Finally reaching the open door to the control room I slithered in and waited. The green glow of the control panel came into focus. Raising up on my hands and knees, I slowly reached the top of the panel and began to turn the knobs hoping to find one that would turn on the lights.

The chamber flooded with light. Ever so cautiously, I eased my way back to the open door and looked out. The floor was a bloody mess and dead bodies seemed to be everywhere. Frantically I searched for Running-water and Al. They were not among the bodies on the floor. It was Saint-Michaels' body that I had crawled over. He was dead. The six other bodies all dressed in black and had black hoods over their heads were dead. I pulled off one hood. It was Kim Su! Then I heard:

"Get the hell off me. Let me up."

"Okay. I was just trying to save your ass." Al said.

"Man, did you just fart?"

"No, but someone sure shit his pants. Whew!" Al said.

"Running-water? Al? Where are you?

A panel slid open and my two sputtering friends emerged.

"Damn! What a mess. You sure can shoot. Remind me never to tangle with you again," Al said.

"You okay, Adam?" Running-water said.

"Fine. Saint-Michaels is dead. I guess we better call the local authorities. There will be a lot of questions."

"Running-water, give me your guns," Al said.

"No way."

"Stop being a big shot and give me those goddamn guns."

"Why do you want his guns?" I asked.

"I live here. You two don't. I know how they work things here. As Saint-Michaels' body guard, I killed these scum bags. My prints need to be on the guns. Gather up the spent shells. I need to handle those as well. The local police will arrive shortly. Odora would have called them by now. They'll come by boat. In the meantime, the two of you go back to the main lobby."

"Speaking of Odora, where is she?" I asked.

"If she has followed drill instructions she is well hidden," Al said.

"Better find her," I said.

"Yeah, guess I better."

"Hey, you big ape, you been holding out on us? Look at the tough guy blush," Running-water laughed.

A few minutes later Odora met us at the elevator as we exited into the public room. She was pale and frightened.

"Al will be right up. Dr. Saint-Michaels is dead as is Kim Su. Have you called the police?" I asked.

"Yes, Mr. Adam. They are on their way."

She was about to say something else when the familiar whirring of a chopper made itself known. We went out onto the front portico. It was Dutch coming in from the airport. He set it down facing the portico and with the ease of a cat, he was out of the chopper and on a full run toward the main house, an Uzi slung over one shoulder and another at the ready.

"I heard on the scanner there was a commotion out here. What's the story?"

Al arrived just as I completed telling Dutch what had transpired. He was carrying a large bag.

"Can't guess what I found down in the hanger?" Al said handing me the bag.

It was full of money.

"The captain of the trawler with some of his men came back. They were in
cahoots with Kim Su and wanted this place to set up a smuggling operation," Al said.

"How do you know that?" Running-water said.

"One of them talked just before I put him out of his misery."

"It would be a good idea if you put that bag out of sight. The police might think it odd that a security guard would have that kind of money. Why don't you just take care of it permanently? A retirement gift," I said.

"Be a good girl, and take care of this for us, will you?" Al said as he handed the bag to Odora. "I've still got some work to do. Adam, all my life I've tried to please people and it never seemed to bring me respect and acceptance until now. Thank you."

"Al, it's okay to be a people pleaser as long as you take time out to please yourself, to think of yourself, and to give value to yourself. If you don't do that you are no more than a slave to the whims of others," I said.

Without comment, he left and went down to the beach, met the local police officers, brought them up to the resonating chamber, and explained to them it was an attempted robbery. Once introductions were completed, the captain was ushered into the main house. The hospitality of the place was offered. Odora brought in fresh fruit, cheeses, and a rum cocktail. Satisfied with the answers we gave and the explanation provided by Al, the captain said he would arrange for the removal of the bodies.

Saint-Michaels would be cremated.

Running-water, Dutch, and I left via the chopper and headed back to the airport where we boarded the jet. On board, I sent Al a message giving him instructions for taking care of the place if he and Odora wanted the job as caretakers.

Maybe someday I would return but not in the immediate future. Right now I had to figure out the meaning of the message, *Be as shifting sand*.

CHAPTER 7 - TEARLESS

A friend is, as it were, a second self.
Aristotle

Morning finally came and as we flew out over the water, it was as though she wanted to apologize for the nastiness of yesterday. Mother Nature rewarded us with a plethora of red-reds and orange pinks thrown up against azure blue and reflected back at us from the mirror-like water below. The total tranquility of it all was in sharp contrast to the carnage we left behind.

The blood and the smell of urine expelled as men died would be a permanent etching on my memory. I was grateful for my friend who once again saved my life but more for the fact that both he and Al had survived. In spite of challenges he presented as a person, the death of Saint-Michaels saddened me. The world will never know or enjoy the benefits of his research because whatever it entailed he kept in his head. There were no notes or records for others to pick up and follow.

The Institute of Light Sciences Technologies will be dissolved and the property and its contents assigned back to Esaugetuh's holdings. Actually, I guess they are my holdings but I still think of myself as a temporary custodian

"Adam, you okay? You haven't said a word since we were airborne. You seem depressed," Running-water said.

"I am deeply concerned about all of these killings, the deaths of all those men. When will it end? The violence is not what I should be about. How many is it now?"

"Twelve men have died and one woman. Thirteen people," Running-water said.

"A blood bath, a carnage. I'm sick of it. It has to stop!"

"You told me of Esaugetuh's fight with the bear. Did he not defend you as well as himself?"

"Yes, but he didn't kill the bear."

"No, but you did. You did protecting yourself and the cougar, therefore, am I a cold blooded killer because I protected you and myself? Am I nothing more than a killing machine as far as you are concerned?"

Suddenly I realized what a terrible thing I was doing, laying blame and guilt on my friend, the very man who was willing to die for me. What an ass! Shame and regret chocked me.

"Oh, man! Here I am wallowing in self-pity and laying a whole lot of crap on you. I apologize, my friend, " I said as I got up, and gave him a bear hug. " My god, Running-water, I am grateful and one damn lucky man to have you as my friend."

"Maybe I am a killer. I don't know, Adam. I do know that I am to make sure you are safe no matter the cost—it's my destiny. I know and you know it. Yes, it bothers me that all these people have died. I remind you that we did not ask them to pursue us, to track us down like animals, and to try to kill us. We are in a defensive situation and that is what we must change."

"You're right. Let's begin again with the message left on the wall at Saint-Michaels'. Do you have the slightest clue as to what that phrase means? Because of all that has happened, I wonder if it was just a ploy by Saint-Michaels to impress us."

"Well, for once I don't think so. Al and I were both with him in the control room and he touched nothing. I guess what we need to do is to analyze what each word means and see where that leads."

"Okay. Let's take the first two words together: 'Be as 'means to exist as something. The word *shifting* describes the action of the sand. Sand moves, creating new forms and new shapes on the desert landscape," I said.

"True, but none of those shapes and forms is permanent. Change seems to me to be the key. The question now becomes change to or for what?" Running-water said.

"We changed the order of people on the list. Even though it seems like a simple thing to do, maybe we should change the sequence again," I said.

"Okay. Who's left on the list?"

"Four people. Jesse was first, Marrie second, Saint-Michaels was the seventh. If we randomly select the next person whoever is behind this will not know that."

I wrote the names on small pieces of paper and placed them in a container, and shook it. Running-water, with eyes closed, selected one. It contained the name, Jedediah Woods. I took it and the other three pieces of paper to the head and flushed them down the toilet.

"Can you can find out about Jedediah Woods on your computer?"

"That's it!" Running-water said, standing up and pulling down his

computer from the overhead compartment.

"What?"

"That's how they know what we are doing. My computer has been hacked. Damn!"

"But we bought a new lap top in Arizona. How can that be hacked?" I asked.

"I'm using the same server, browser, and password as I've used all along."

"Can you fix that?"

"Yes, when we land."

"Better fasten up. We are approaching Miami International." Dutch announced.

The navigator came into the main cabin and told us that we would have to go through customs. They would come on board and this news made Running-water nervous.

"Where's the duffel with all that cash?" Running-water asked.

"Just above your head. Why?"

"The Customs people just might make a thorough search and we'd have to explain a lot of things that we may not want to reveal right now."

"And what about your extra set of guns?"

"I have a permit to carry concealed weapons. And since this is a private plane, I don't think they will be an issue. What do you want to do with the money?"

"There's a security box as part of the headboard of the bed. Stow it in there. Bring the duffle back to me. We'll put my camera, your lap top, and a couple books in it."

That done we settled into our chairs for the final approach and touchdown. Dutch taxied up to our designated gate and waited for further instructions. He greeted two agents who boarded the plane and escorted them back to where Running-water and I sat. Each of us identified who we were as we showed our driver's licenses and passports. Running-water briefly explained that we were returning from a sad trip, the death of Dr. Christopher Saint-Michaels who worked for my foundation.

"And why have you landed here rather than at your point of origin?" asked one of the two agents.

"We filed a change in flight plans before we left the island," Dutch said.

"That doesn't answer my question."

"My computer has been hacked and I need to fix it. This is the closest point for us to land." Running-water said.

"You mean a virus? That doesn't sound like a reason to divert the plane's destination."

"No, not a virus. Someone has accessed my files and has transferred my protocol to another computer. Because all of our business records are on the computer, they are now available to whoever broke into the computer. I need to do a complete wipe of the machine, reformat, reload all the software then my files, and change servers. As you know we can't use our computer while in flight."

"How are you going to reload your files if you have to wipe your computer clean?" said the other agent.

"Ah, back-up copies. There, in the duffle." Running-water said pointing above his head.

"Too complicated for me. How long will you be here?"

"We don't plan to lay over if that's what you mean? A few hours at the most."

"Do you have anything to declare?"

"No, as I said we were at a funeral."

"Have a safe flight, gentlemen." The agent said as he and his partner left the plane.

"You got a destination in mind?" Dutch said.

"No. I'll let you know later. Arrange to refuel the plane. Use this card. Right now I need to get off the plane and walk around."

While Running-water was doing his thing with his computer, I took a slow walk throughout the terminal trying to determine an explanation and meaning of the message burned into the wall of the resonating chamber. It's true sand shifts, changes and creates new patterns. Sand is miniscule, yet it has shape, dimension, even weight. Its shape reveals the distance it has traveled. It may be quartz and feldspar, volcanic or shell in composition. Some sands are used in making glass. Glass can be seen through, molded into an infinite number of shapes and colors. It can be shattered, melted down, and reused.

No, get away from the glass analogy. It's the movement of the sand that holds the key. Shifting. One shifts gears, shifts positions. Shifting sand changes. Change what? Change location, the sequence of names on the list, change identities? Questions, more questions, and no answers.

I stopped at one of the coffee shops. Ordered a coffee. I watched the waiter fill a salt shaker and that brought me back to my analysis.

The sand moves, flows with the wind and puts up no resistance. Flow, no resistance! Of course, Prometheus and Necessity. [9] Why didn't I think of that earlier? Okay, so I must act out of Necessity. Esaugetuh liked to remind me that the canoe paddle was used to guide the canoe on its journey, not to create the journey. And like all rivers, there are jutties, rocks, and other dangers. This journey, like the flow of a river, has pitfalls also: the names on a list, the cabalistic message, the disappearance of Esaugetuh, and the all those deaths. They will haunt me forever. Maybe I need to go home. Home! My god, How could I have forgotten?.

Guilty uneasiness pushed its way to the surface of my being. How long had it been since I had talked to my parents? Two years? Closer to three? I whipped out the cell phone and punched in the numbers. A voice came on line telling me the number was no longer in service.

"What the hell," I said.

"Sir? Something wrong with your coffee?"

"No. No. Cell phone issue."

I called Jacquelyn, my former fiancée. Her mother answered the phone.

I thought she had fainted because of the long pause.

"Where—where are you? Everyone thinks you're dead."

"Well, I'm not. I tried calling my parents but the phone had been disconnected. What's going on?"

"Oh my, I don't know quite how to say this. I'm so sorry, Adam. Your parents were killed in a tragic car accident."

"Accident? What happened?"

"There's some question as to the cause, but I really don't know the details. You know, Jacquelyn has married. Married a lawyer. Fine young man."

"No, I didn't. Congratulate her for me. I wish her much happiness. Can you give me my parent's attorney's number?"

My conversation with my parents' attorney wasn't what I had expected. His tone and lack of sincerity set up my warning flags. I told him my attorney would be in touch regarding my parents' estate. He seemed so agitated.

It bothered me that had I shed no tears on learning of my parents' deaths and that surprised me but then again, I'm not the same man as I was when I left their home. A stranger in a strange land, is that what I have become? A wanderer without roots, actually homeless. Am I to spend my days wandering, nomadic, and aimless? Is that the way it was for Esaugetuh? At least I have a friend. As Kipling so aptly put it, *the thousandth man will follow you to the grave and after*. Running-water is that thousandth man without question.

A voice from far off my conscious map finally penetrated my mind. It was Dutch. I was so deep in my self-interrogation it hadn't at first registered he had spoken to me.

" Been looking for you. Running-water says he's got the computer fixed. We need to get a runway assigned and take off. You decided where we're going?"

"No. I'll know more after I talk with Running-water.

***

"It took a little doing after I took care of the hacking problem, but I think I've located our man. He's in Pennsylvania," Running-water said.

"Got an address?"

"Yes, however, the nearest airport is at Williamsport, fifty miles from where he lives. You want me to rent a car?" Running-water said.

"Hold off on the car. Give Dutch the location of the airport so he can make preparations for our departure. I want to talk to you privately."

"I called home and there was no answer. I called a family friend and was told my parents were killed in a car accident."

"Oh, man. That sucks. You want to go to where they lived instead of Williamsport?"

"No. What has struck me is I shed no tears. There just weren't any. Don't you think it strange that I feel no sense of loss or grief? What the hell has happened to me? Have I become so inhuman that I no longer feel? Has whatever took place in the woods at Tahoe made me into an automaton, unfeeling and cold?"

"Of course not. Each man grieves in his own way and in his own time. Tears are not required. Memories will come as ghosts in the night; you will know their meaning."

"I feel I am surrounded by death; it stalks me, waiting for me to provide its next prey. Speaking of prey, I would like you to do something for me. Take care of my parents' estate. I feel their attorney is not too happy that I'm alive. It's just something about his tone of voice."

"Consider it done. No problem."

"Here's his name and number. Make sure you get an accounting of every dime, even the funerary expenses. At some point, I need to go back there, open the house, and take care of some things and put the house up for sale. Perhaps we can go there after we see Mr. Jedediah Woods."

"By the way, I didn't mention that Jedediah has several degrees including a doctorate in philosophy. He's never married. He's very much a hermit. Wonder how Esaugetuh tied in with him?"

"Interesting. I note that two people were *uneducated* and now Jedediah makes two that are *educated,*" I said.

"What's the point of the uneducated-educated comment?" Running-water asked.

" I'm still trying to find a pattern to all of this. Educated is such a relative term. College degrees do not always denote an educated person. I'm sure you've met a few who have had degrees and didn't know jack rabbit. As far as I know, Esaugetuh holds no degrees yet he is one of the most lucid, erudite, and cultured men I have ever known. Each of those on our list has provided wisdom and insights. Education comes in many forms. I wonder if it's possible that the purpose of the list is to have me, or rather us, learn something new, a life-lesson."

"Speaking of life's lessons, and I hate to bring this up, Adam, I've learned one. If I don't work, no money. I'm flat broke. I have to go back to New Mexico and get back to work."

"Oh, man. I am dumb. Stay with me. I'll put you on an exclusive contract and speaking of contracts, what kind of deal do I have with the pilot and navigator?"

"I really don't know. My uncle sent them. He's an attorney, also."

" Can't have them walking out on us. Divide the cash that's in the safe between the three of you. And find out if I owe them more than that. And see if they'd like a permanent job with us."

"With us?"

"Well, yeah. You and me. Unless you aren't accepting my offer of fulltime employment as my attorney."

"Great. I'll see Dutch and Brett right now."

I chewed at Saint-Michaels about not knowing his people. I'm certainly no better. I know nothing about either man. That will be remedied, I thought.

"Well, looks like there's hope for you after all."

"What?" I looked up. No one was there.

CHAPTER 8 - JEDEDIAH WOODS

Be faithful to that which exists nowhere but *in* yourself–and thus make yourself indispensable.
Andre Gide

Our flight was smooth and uneventful. A taxi took us to a motel. After a meal at a burger place, I gave the plane's crew the night off and sent Running-water off for an evening of R&R. I looked forward to some quite time, some alone time

It still bothered me that I had no tears for my parents. Admittedly, my father was aloof and often dismissive, but my mother was warm and nurturing. Another thing that bothered me was the real lack of an attempt to find me. My parents had my cell phone number and it was always on.

Morning brought no sign of my three companions. After a hearty breakfast, I went back to my room, called a rental place, and rented a truck with four wheel drive. I had it delivered to the motel. I drove to a sporting goods store, picked up two sleeping bags, a shotgun, couple boxes of shells, a map, and then stopped back at the motel.

Still no sign of Dutch, Brett, or Running-water. I called their rooms and there was no answer. I asked the desk clerk to check the rooms. It was just as I suspected; they had not slept at the motel. Sure that they found other beds for the night, I decided to head north and to do so without Running-water. After all, I started this journey alone and it was no big deal to continue by myself. At some point in time, Running-water would catch up.

It was just about noon when I arrived in one of those quaint little magazine towns probably dating back to the early 1800's. An old and narrow wooden walkway ran in front of the building. At one end of the walkway and very close to the road stood a gas pump, the kind you cranked to pull the gas up out of the underground tank. I remembered using one of those in Northern Quebec. I went inside, paid for the gas, and got some further directions.

"You going do some fishing? If you are, Pine Creek's a good place. Great rainbows and native browns," the clerk said.

"Yeah. Heard it was a good place."

I headed north and then a few miles later, turned west.

Jedediah Woods lived in Canyon Country. According to my map, the Pennsylvania Grand Canyon dropped a thousand feet at its deepest point and at its bottom was a meandering creek that ran for fifty miles emptying itself into the Susquehanna River. A railroad snaked its way along one side of Pine Creek. Jedediah Woods supposedly lived off from one of the many switchbacks in the area.

In years gone by, snuggled in the Canyon area there had been tanning and lumbering towns. Remnants of the company owned row houses still remained as private summer camps. Names like Blackwell, Cedar Run, Leetonia, and Tiadaghton reflect the history of those industries. About twenty miles down the road, the paved highway became dirt. Spring rains had muddied it and vehicles had created deep ruts making the going anything but smooth. The four wheel drive came in handy because at one point the left front end sank nearly to its fender. Because of my concern about the road, I nearly missed my turn-off. The lush overgrown brush didn't help matters.

I was forced to ease my way along; the road was little more than a path covered with over hanging tree branches, tentacles of blackberry bushes and budded dogwood trees. A good twenty minutes later and without warning, I came out into a beautiful meadow filled with wild flowers of every imaginable color.

A considerable distance from the meadow entrance and on a gentle knoll sat a log cabin. It was about 24X48 feet with a lean-to filled with neatly stacked wood on the south end of the cabin. It was a perfect Thomas Kinkaid painting. A single shuttered window faced the road.

Easing my way closer to the cabin, I could see several fruit trees in bloom. Their color suggested they were apple trees. Just to the right of these was a plot of freshly plowed earth. A hand plow stood sentry in the middle of an incomplete furrow.

Following the path, I drove the truck around to the back of the cabin and there, sitting on the porch was a man that could be sixty or eighty years old. He was one of those people who was probably born old, his physical appearance not having changed in forty years. Wisps of snow white hair covered his head and a very long beard, covering most of his face, stained at the mouth from years of chewing tobacco. He was a Rip Van Winkle personified.

"Hello, I'm Adam," I said getting out of the truck.

"I know. I've been waiting for you." Jedediah said.

"You have?"

"Esaugetuh said you'd come by. Said you'd have someone with you. I see you're alone."

"You know about Running-water?"

"Don't know a name. Just that you'd have someone with you that I should meet. That Esaugetuh sure was a mystery. Come sit yourself down. Going to be a nice sunset this evening. Won't be long before the deer come to feed. I put a salt-lick out for them along with a tub of water."

"How is it you know Esaugetuh?"

"We go back quite a long time. Can't recollect how many years it's been. We met at a meeting on Indian affairs. Ha! What a joke! It was really white man's affairs put on to the Indian. Anyway, he was one of the speakers. He so impressed me with his insights, simply stated and yet poetically profound. Even the dumbest political ass there could understand. In fact, as I recall, I was so impressed that I went up to him and told him so. After that, we spent several hours talking. Each year for several years thereafter, we would meet at the conferences. Then he stopped coming to the conferences. I stopped going because I realized I only went because he was going to be there. About three years ago he came here to see me, a shot right out of the blue."

"What did he want?"

"We'll talk later. Watch the deer. See how their ears twitch. They are listening to us. Sometimes one or two will come right up to the porch and take a carrot from my hand."

We sat in a comfortable silence as the sun slid from view and shadow fingers began to stalk the meadow. Sweet smells of apple and clover filled the air as the cacophonic songs of insects punctuated by the booming voice of bull frogs competed for my attention. Rabbits scurried about, nibbling here and there. Darkness fell and I was sure my host was sleeping in his chair. I was mistaken.

"When Esaugetuh was here, they would come and talk to him. Ah, yes, but that was then and this is now. Time to go in. Soup's on. You'll be staying awhile." Jedediah said as he raised his bent frame up from his chair. "You'll have to sleep on the floor. I got an extra blanket."

"I have a sleeping bag with me."

If he could have stood straight up, I was sure he would have been close to seven feet tall. As he turned to go into the cabin, his bent torso was nearly at right angles to the ground. He did not appear to be in pain as he walked.

Inside at the far end of the room and taking up the major portion of the wall was a large fieldstone fireplace with a huge wooden mantel running the full width of the wall. A large cast-iron pot, blackened from years of use, hung on a hook just above the fire pit. Whatever kind of soup was simmering in that pot it sure was tantalizing and I was hungry.

Hanging along the fireplace on metal hooks were a large frying pan, a second frying pan, smaller in size, and two other very black pots also smaller than the one over the fire pit. Just inside the fireplace sat a coffee pot, the kind that boils the coffee rather than perking it. Steam lazily eased its way out of its lidless top and gently mixed with the smoke from the glowing embers.

In the center of the room, hanging from a heavy chain fastened to a beam in the open ceiling was a huge wagon wheel with a dozen spikes sticking straight up. Each contained a homemade candle. Jedediah lowered the wheel and lit four of the candles. Their radiance shone down upon an old oak table whose top was at least four inches thick. A three legged stool was at one end and along one side was a split log bench. The table was set with three plates, three bowls, three cups, and flatware. It was obvious he was expecting me and it was just as obvious that he had been expecting me for quite some time. Two sets of dishes, those sitting in front of the split log bench, were dust laden. Jedediah noticed and brushed them off with a piece of old towel that had seen better days. He served up the soup, large hunks of homemade bread, and a sharp cheese. Once he sat down, he bowed his head and said, "Unto thee O Lord."

"Amen," I said.

It had been a long time since I had heard a grace given before a meal. Its simplicity and the sincerity in which it was said moved me and reminded me of the days on the road with Esaugetuh. He used to say a prayer over the game he had killed for our dinner.

The soup was great. Jedediah called it root soup.

During our meal, we sat in silence so I had time to notice that his eyes were pitch black. They gave me the distinct impression that there was an endless depth there and unlike those of Esaugetuh, they didn't penetrate. Eyes say so little yet tell so much when observed and in this case, they were a blank shield, impenetrable, protective of that which lay beneath.

Chewing on a hunk of bread I wondered what kind of man he was. I continued to gaze around the room and noticed there was no telephone, no television, no radio, and no computer present. One wall was a giant floor to ceiling bookcase and it was crammed with books. More books filled the loft. Along the wall, by the fireplace, was a bunk bed made of animal skins stretched over four log poles driven into the earthen floor. Opposite the bed, on the other side of the fireplace, sat a hand carved rocking chair surrounded by piles of books stacked on old orange crates, and a small table with a kerosene lamp. Thoreau would have considered this place a palace. A bushel basket in one corner really caught my attention. I got up from the bench to take a closer look. It contained framed diplomas and sheepskins covered with years of dust.

"Why don't you have your diplomas and degrees hanging on the wall?" I asked.

"Why should I?"

"They represent a certain level of achievement."

"I know what I have or have not achieved. I don't need a piece of paper to tell me that."

"But you went through all the trouble and necessary steps to get them. At some point, they must have had meaning?" I insisted.

"Just jumping through the hoop; that's all it represents. What's important is right here in these books. I don't need an institution to tell me to read them."

"You've read all of these books?"

"Yes and some of them several times."

"And what good has all of that done you?"

"Don't really know. Say, you sure are full of questions aren't you? Esaugetuh said you had a penchant for asking questions."

"And what good has all of that done others? Isn't this some kind of an ego trip?"

"Humph."

"Well, isn't it?" I said.

"Self-knowledge is never an ego trip," Jedediah said.

"And all of these books have provided you self-knowledge?"

"I'm not sure we are talking about the same thing no—no, they haven't. What do you mean by self-knowledge?" Jedediah said.

I had to lean back as he jabbed his finger at me.

His hands were large hands, roughhewn and strong telling the tale of many hours of digging in the earth, felling trees, chopping kindling, and planting crops. There was just a slight tremor in the finger he was pointing at me.

"I don't think you can find self-knowledge in books," I said.

"You haven't answered my question, what do you mean by self-knowledge?"

"I'm talking about who we are, what we are; those understandings of Self that come through self-examination."

"Don't tell me we are going to play the ten and twenty Socratic questions? Good heavens, I thought most moderns were beyond all that." Jedediah said.

"If you are referring to Socrates' 'A life unexamined is not worth living.' I most certainly am not."

"Might be some hope for you after all. Have a cup of coffee?"

"Sure."

He got up from the table, got the coffee pot, stopped, and picked up a small jug that sat by the rocking chair. He poured from both into each cup.

"Good old fashioned corn. It'll do you good. Come let's sit a spell on the porch and watch the stars. I find that a very peaceful thing to do."

A chill had settled in and a light dew began to fall. Even though it was only mid-March the coolness didn't seem to bother Jedediah. Above and stretching out as far as the eye could see was a skyline filled with billions of glowing lights. I could see them winking at one another as they whispered celestial mysteries across the vast universe. An owl hooted in the distance and I heard fast moving feet.

"Deer," Jedediah said.

We sat there quiet, each off in whatever world our minds created. Jedediah finally broke the silence.

"Guess you better get your sleeping bag so it has a chance to warm up."

I got the bag, picked up the shotgun, shells, backpack, and phone. Inside Jedediah gave me a kerosene lamp with the warning not to go to sleep with it still burning. The loft was mine. It took a couple of trips up the ladder to get my gear up there because books were everywhere. Instead of the oil lamp, I used a battery powered light I brought with me. I shoved stacks of books and magazines aside and soon had the bed roll laid out.

I turned off the light and wondered if we really have to accept our illusions. Is that all we have? Seems to me the danger lies in not realizing they are illusions, making us dependent, slave-like, to an imaginary world. Peggy Lee's "Is that all there is?" floated through my mind as I drifted off to sleep.

Morning brought the need to relieve myself. It wasn't quite daylight. I hadn't noticed a bathroom so I guess it would be necessary for me to go outdoors to relieve myself. Having slept in my clothes I crawled out of the sleeping bag and eased my way down the ladder.

"Morning. There's a toilet behind the lean-to. The fire will soon warm the place. Breakfast will be ready by the time you get back."

It was an outhouse, a two holer. Even had a crescent moon cut in the door. I hadn't seen one of these since I was a kid during my Canadian days. At least there was toilet paper. Back in the cabin, Jedediah pointed out a sink that I had not noticed the night before. It was wooden and had a pump for water, the kind you prime. I found the soap and a towel neatly laid out for me. The water was ice cold. It wasn't until after I nearly froze my face off that I saw a small basin with hot water in it. Talk about being dumb.

"You sure are a dumb one. Don't know a thing about taking care of yourself."

"It's been awhile," I said laughing.

Breakfast was something else. Homemade cornmeal flapjacks, lots of real maple syrup. Eggs had never tasted so good.

"Where's this friend of yours, the one you call Running-water?"

"I really don't know. He didn't sleep at the motel where we stayed. I assume he met a woman and is off somewhere with her. I have to admit it is not like Running-water not to stay in touch."

"What's he to you?"

"He's my attorney. No, more than that. Much more. He's my friend and I am lucky to have such a man as a friend."

"He's a Native American?"

"Yes. He belongs to one of the tribes in the southwest. I think he's Apache." I said.

"What do you know about him? His family, relatives?" Jedediah said.

"I know he has a twin sister who works in the Bureau of Indian Affairs in Washington. Beyond that, I know nothing."

"And you call this man friend? How can that be when you do not know him?"

"When you have shared death with a man, you don't need to know anything more about him than how he behaved. That's the only measure necessary. You certainly don't need to know a person's pedigree to call him friend."

"Yet, you think that displaying my degrees will tell you about me? My achievements, as you called them. Isn't that the reason you think I should display them?"

"No! I questioned you to determine why you did not display them since you had earned them. And since you answered it was not necessary because you knew what you had or had not achieved, I wondered why you had bothered to keep them around if they had no meaning to you."

"Meaning is a relative term," Jedediah said.

"And so is life." I snapped.

"Actually, you are absolutely correct. Each individual life has meaning or relevancy only to that individual. Oh, society attempts to give meaning by calling for contributions and sacrifices and then giving recognition to those very things that it has demanded. You know the kind of thing I'm talking about: the plaques, certificates, honorary degrees, banquets, and testimonials. The more famous and infamous get their stories told on television, in books, and movies."

"Okay, I'll give you that for now, but what is it that gives your own life meaning or relevancy?" I said.

"You always ask such questions?" Jedediah said.

Just for a moment, I thought I saw a spark in his dark eyes. It was as though a glimmer of life had returned. Is that why I'm here? To bring life back to this old man? What did Esaugetuh have in mind by telling Jedediah that there would be someone with me, someone of interest? The questions continued to race through my mind.

"Being here in this place, at this time, gives me great peace and comfort," Jedediah said, finally breaking the silence between us.

"And this peace and comfort have given your life meaning? It has created in you a sense of personal worth and dignity?"

"No. No! It's all a god damned lie. There's no meaning to my life. I get up, take a crap, eat, work in the garden, read books, eat, get drunk on homemade hooch, take a piss, go to bed, and start all over again the next day. How in the hell can anyone call that meaningful?"

"Why?"

"Why? I can't answer that." Jedediah said.

"Can't? Won't? Afraid to? Which is it?"

"Esaugetuh told me a poem many years ago that asked the question 'What is life?'" [10]

"It is the flash of a firefly in the night." I recited.

Jedediah completed the line, *"It is the breath of a buffalo in the winter time, It is the little shadow that runs across the grass and loses itself in the sunset."*

"And you, Jedediah Woods are that little shadow that runs across the grass and loses itself. You have lost your sense of Self," I said.

"How long do you plan on staying?"

The hostility in his voice even though he spoke quietly was very evident. I couldn't read anything in his eyes to help me formulate an answer. I wondered if he was that dead inside or was it a game.

"Well? I asked you a question," Jedediah said.

"That you did. I guess I stay until you get tired of my questions and kick me out."

"Well, one thing is for sure. We can't sit around here all day and shoot the fat. I have work to do and you can just get busy and help. You ever plow a field?"

"No."

"Today you will and then we'll see how many questions you ask."

He gave the challenge. I knew nothing about farming. One thing was for sure, Jedediah Woods was going to work my ass off and enjoy every moment of it. We went out to the garden.

"See that plow. You put the harness on and pull it. I'll follow with the cultivator. You can walk a straight line?"

Ignoring his sarcasm, I eased myself into the harness, placing a strap over each shoulder. I began to pull the plow. It seemed to be stuck so I really put myself into it. The plow came loose, tipping end over end and smacked me in the middle of my back. I went down. It knocked the wind out of me. I was sure it broke my back in half.

"I guess you have a lot to learn after all. Next time, when the blade is stuck, go back and see why. You're lucky you didn't have your head taken off."

Jedediah didn't offer to help me up. I managed to get myself up and back into the harness. I was determined not to let him get the best of me. I'd show him.

I thought, now who's on an ego trip. Esaugetuh would really chew my ass out. Okay, relax. Enjoy the beauty of the day; drink in the experience of the earth, and just do your best.

I felt Jedediah's eyes boring into my back.

By the fifth furrow, I had established a reasonable rhythm despite my back and shoulders aching as they had never ached before. I had also learned that weights were required on the back of the plow and the number of weights determined the depth of the furrow.

We worked past any lunch time and on into the sunset. I was sure his intent was to kill me off. Finally, he said it was time to quit. I staggered like a drunk back to the cabin. I sat down on the bench and put my head down on the table all the while thinking he had won. I heard him dragging something and was sure it was a box to put my body in.

"Here, drink this. It's good for you. I'm heating you some hot water and you can tub soak. It'll relax those aching muscles."

It didn't take long for the whiskey to kick in. I had not eaten since early morning. That stuff must have been 150 proof.

"Get your clothes off. Test the water first. It's hot. Ease yourself into the tub." Jedediah said.

The tub was a huge pot. I'd seen pictures of such a pot used for scalding pigs after they had been killed and bled. The water was hot but I gradually got my whole being into the water. It was wonderful. The heat of the water, the heat of the fireplace, and the heat of the whiskey did their work. Sleep. Rough hands working my shoulders and the smell of some kind of liniment woke me.

"Easy. You fell asleep."

"What is that awful smell?" I mumbled.

"Horse liniment. Best thing in the world for bruised shoulders. Lean forward. Let me see your back. You have one hell of a black and blue mark. Covers the whole of your back. That'll most likely give you some trouble. Supper's about ready. Here's a blanket, wrap yourself in that and come to table."

Baked beans and they were delicious. Two plates, three large hunks of bread and a sugar pudding of some kind finally abated my hunger.

"You're a good looking young man. You got a woman somewhere?" Jedediah said.

"What? No, no I don't, not anymore. She's married someone else now. Can't blame her. I've been gone a long time." I said.

"How about you? You got a lady friend?"

"Did once. Not anymore. What have you accomplished today? What is it you feel? Has it been meaningful? Do you think you have shown me you could take it?"

"Well, I did get a good number of rows plowed. That was an accomplishment and I feel good about that. I guess you could say that it was meaningful because it gave me personal satisfaction." I said.

"And is it acceptable to derive personal satisfaction from accomplishing something?"

"Of course."

"Then why do you criticize me if I feel a personal satisfaction in creating my own home, providing for most of my own food?"

"Uh-uh, not so fast. Not only are you switching words on me, you have also switched subjects. I did not criticize you for creating your own home and providing your own food. Meaningful and satisfaction are two different words."

"Okay. We'll come back to that. What about my other question? Do you think you have shown me you could take it?"

"I have to admit that it was my original intent. I was really going to show you but then it changed."

"Can you pinpoint the time or circumstance when it changed?"

"Hmm. I guess it was after the plow knocked me down and I realized your work depended upon me getting mine done."

"An interesting answer. Glad to hear you admit that you were pissed enough to want to show me up." Jedediah said as he got up from his stool, stripped his clothes off, and hobbled over to the tub, and poured in more hot water.

"What are you doing now?" I said.

"What do you think it looks like? I'm taking a bath."

"But you didn't empty the tub and put in clean water."

"So what. Your dirt is the same as mine. Same field."

I had to laugh at the logic but what the heck. It's his house and I'm his guest. If he wants to conserve water, fine with me. His bent back bothered me. I wondered if he had ever gone to have it checked. I noticed no scars from any surgeries. Had he always been bent? Perhaps that is the reason for his self-imposed exile. While he was taking his bath, he treated me to a medley of whistled songs.

When he emerged from his 'soak' I said, "What happened to your back? Have you always been crippled?"

"It was a gradual thing. Started in my late 40's. Went to a doctor once. He told me there was nothing that could be done except wear a brace. I wasn't wearing any damn brace. Why do you want to know?"

"Do you mind if I try something? It just may help." I said.

"What are you going to do?

"You'll see. Just stand still. You will begin to feel intense heat. Don't be alarmed."

Placing both hands just above his buttocks, thumbs together, and fingers spread out toward each of his sides I gradually brought heat to my hands. As the heat intensified, Saint-Michaels came to mind. I saved his life only to have it snuffed out with a bullet. What will be the result of my efforts here? Because of the negative thoughts, there was a quick and noticeable cooling in my hands. Negative feelings and thoughts are not conducive to healing.

I quieted my mind and the heat returned to my hands and grew strong again.

"When I count to five I want you to try and straighten up. Can you do that for me?" I said.

"Count."

On five, he straightened about two inches and cried out. My hands began to cool. Evidently, my own injuries were requiring my energy to heal them.

"How do you feel?" I asked.

"Like a truck had just run over me. What the hell did you do? My skin felt like it was on fire."

"I'm a healer. Tomorrow we'll try again. I'm not up to full strength. The blow to my back is sucking my energy. Explain what you felt when you yelled."

"It was like I had been stabbed with a knife."

"Exactly where was the pain?"

"Right about where your thumbs were. That's important?"

"It tells me where to begin again tomorrow. I think that bunk of yours needs to have the hides stretched again or have them replaced. There's a big sag in the middle and that doesn't help your back."

"Do you have a last name?" Jedediah said as he eased himself into his rocking chair.

I went over, put a small log on the fire, and poured him a drink from the jug.

"I have another name given to me by Esaugetuh. In Sioux, my name is Ikæe wicasa and it means *original man*."

"That you are, that you are!" Jedediah said as he dozed off.

I went out to the back porch and sat down on the one step. It was a clear night, still, and about 45 degrees. A shooting star graced the heavens with its moment of light.

Continuing my skyward gaze, I counted seven shooting stars. Seven is an important sign for Esaugetuh, his people, and has become one for me. Are there not seven continents? What meaning lies within this incident of seven I don't know? Whatever it has I sensed it was a good time to meditate. I got up from the porch step, meandered out to the open field, sat down, Indian style, and began to empty my mind letting whatever thoughts came to go unexamined.

Loneliness filled my soul and with its departure came emptiness, absolute and complete. Despair cried out and total helplessness flooded my being as the realization that hope was gone settled over me. Without hope, there is nothing, absolutely nothing except a living death. It was emanating from the cabin.

I was experiencing the private and personal pain of Jedediah Woods. Something interrupted the sensations I was experiencing. Perhaps it was the call of the goatsucker in the nearby woods. I shivered and realized I was stark naked and hustled my butt back into the cabin, picking up my blanket on the step as I did so. The warmth of the fire felt good. I put a small log on the fire, adjusted the blanket on Jedediah, then climbed the ladder, and went to bed. Tomorrow would be different.

***

The smell of freshly brewed coffee wafting up to the loft tantalized my nose into waking me. I still felt a little stiff as I eased my way down the ladder. Jedediah was cooking home fries. He seemed to be standing straighter. I would try healing again after breakfast.

But before we sat down he said, "I want to look at your back and shoulders."

I pulled off my shirt.

"My god there isn't a mark on your back. What are you?

"I told you. I'm a healer."

"That you are. Unto thee," he said, head bowed.

"Jedediah, I want to try another healing session on your back if it's okay with you?"

"Can't say that it did any harm. Go ahead."

Once he had removed his bibbed overalls and his shirt, I asked him to place both hands on the table. Again, I placed my hands on his back but this time I placed the heels of my hands where my thumbs had been before and applied a gentle and continuous pressure. My hands reddened as the heat began to flow into his back.

"When your back feels really hot, let me know."

"It's getting hot."

"When you feel it burning hot slowly straighten up. Slowly, Jedediah."

He straightened and cried out at the same time. I kept my hands in place, lessening the pressure while moving them in clockwise motions and then removed them completely.

"Jedediah there will be no field work for you today or the next several days. It's also necessary to put a poultice on your back. I need to go out into the fields and woods to look for some natural medicines. While I'm gone, do not lift anything, not even a dish. You understand! You could undo everything. Then there will be nothing more I can do. Will you do as I ask?"

"Only under protest, but I'll do it."

I began what turned out to be a very long walk, taking my time looking for just the right shrubs, bushes, and plants. Several hours later, with my gunny sack full, I returned to the cabin.

Jedediah was anxiously waiting for me.

"What did you get?"

"Mullen and Juniper leaves, Balsam Fir gum, wild horseradish and mustard and a few herbs. Some will be ground up, cooked in water until they become a thick paste. Others I'll use to make a tea for you to drink. The paste, once on your back, will have to be covered. You got an old shirt you don't want?"

"Sure. There's an old flannel on the hook by the door. Use that."

After my assortment of plants was ground up and put to cook, I tackled Jedediah's bunk. It took a good deal of effort to make the deer skins taut and to lace them back to their posts. Finally, they were tight enough. A quarter would bounce on them. A firm support was necessary for Jedediah's back. It was unlikely that he would ever be totally straight but he wouldn't be kissing the ground when he walked.

The aroma of juniper mixed with balsam filled the cabin giving it a renewed freshness. While the poultice simmered, I made the herbal tea using wintergreen leaves, spikenard, and Echinacea leaves. For good measure, I spiked it with a hefty shot of Jedediah's corn whiskey.

"You haven't eaten since early this morning and neither have I. Don't know about you but I'm hungry," Jedediah said.

"No problem. I picked up some Indian turnips, dandelions, and I'll mix those with the tops of the mustard and we'll have some good eating in no time. In the meantime drink this tea." I said.

"Tell me, Adam, where is your friend? You called him Running-water, I believe."

"I really don't know. He didn't sleep in his room at the motel where we stayed. He knows where I am. I'm sure he'll show up. It might be a good idea, however, to check with Dutch and Brett to see if they have seen him."

"Who are they?"

"My pilot and navigator. They're with my plane at Williamsport."

"You own your own plane?"

"Well, actually, it's Esaugetuh's. I'm using it. Food's ready." I said.

"Not bad. The tea is another matter." Jedediah said as he slurped up the last morsel on his plate with a hunk of bread and sloshed it down with the rest of the tea.

"Glad you liked it. As soon as the mixture cools down a little more, I'll apply it to your back. In the meantime, I want you to lie down on your stomach and cover up. I'm going to call the plane and see if Dutch knows anything about Running-water."

I couldn't get a connection on my cell phone and I didn't have any better luck outside.

I stayed outside for a while, paced up and down.

I muttered to myself, I could stay put and see if Running-water shows up, go to the hotel where I bought gas and use a phone there, or return to the city. Well hell, he's probably tried to call me and couldn't reach me anymore than I have been able to get a hold of him. Right now Jedediah is my concern. Somehow, I have got to get him to open up. Some kind of an inner despair is destroying him. One thing at a time is a good adage to follow.

Back inside, I stirred the mixture, tested it for heat, and then applied it to Jedediah's back. You would have thought I was killing him the way he put up a fuss.

"Damn it, boy. You trying to cook me alive?"

His cussing blued the air. I managed to get his shirt on and got him wrapped up in a blanket. The tea kicked in and he drifted off to sleep. He should sleep for a few hours.

I went out to the truck, cranked it up, and turned on the radio to a station at Williamsport. There was no news of any murders or missing persons. I plugged the cell phone into the lighter to see if the extra power would help. Still no luck. The lack of communication from Running-water was worrying me. It was not like him. He should have caught up with me by now. Jedediah's interest in him has raised questions. Wonder what Esaugetuh had told him about Running-water?

I busied myself chopping wood and filling up the wood box. After that, I decided that I would make bread. I wondered how Jedediah baked bread. I began to look around. There was an oven built into the fireplace. I found a wooden paddle, a wooden bowl, flour, salt, but no yeast. I was sure bread took yeast.

While I was rummaging around in his one cupboard, I knocked over several cans of beans.

"What in hell are you doing? Tearing my house down?"

"Sorry. I was looking for the yeast to make bread. Can't find any."

"It's in that ceramic pot with a lid on it."

"If you get up, slowly roll on to your side. I'll help you the rest of the way. We'll need to fix you a walking stick so you can use it to get up and to get around for the next few days. How do you feel?"

"Like a cantankerous old coot that has had too much to drink. What did you put in that tea?"

"Glad you're feeling better."

"So you're fixing to bake bread? You know what you are doing. Have you tested the oven to see that it's hot enough?"

"Tested the oven?"

"Of course. You put a stick of hickory in the oven. If it catches fire, the oven is hot enough. What kind of bread are you making?"

"Herb. It'll go with your root soup I'm warming."

"How many loaves you planning on making? The number depends upon how much of the starter you put in."

" Okay, how about four loaves. On the road we made flat bread," I said.

"Your mother teach you how to do that?"

No. Esaugetuh did. You live on the road and in the wilderness, you learn to eat off the land. Speaking of Esaugetuh, what did he tell you about Running-water?"

"He said you would bring someone with you that would be important to me and when I saw him I would know why," Jedediah said, heading out the door.

"Hey, where do you think you are going?" I said.

"To take a piss. Don't tell me you have to help me do that, too?"

"Don't get smart old man. Keep it up and no dinner for you."

I caught a sheepish grin on his face as he slammed the door shut. I placed the rounded loaves on the wooden paddle and shoved it into the oven. I would have to stay alert or the bread would burn up on me. Jedediah returned from his water-letting expedition and was in a much more congenial mood.

"Can you hang that mirror for me? I can stand in front of it now. Don't have to look down at it on the table anymore, thanks to you."

With the mirror now hung, Jedediah actually trimmed his beard and combed back his hair. Then, with my help, he put on clean clothes.

I pulled the piping hot bread from the oven, gave the soup a stir, and prepared to serve it up.

"I got some troubles," Jedediah said.

"Troubles?"

"I'm going to lose this place and the land. Haven't paid the taxes on it. No money. How'd you like to buy it? I'll sell it cheap and you hire me as a caretaker."

"How much in back taxes do you owe?"

"A bunch. When you first came, I thought you might be from the sheriff's office but when you asked about Esaugetuh I knew different."

"How much?" I repeated.

"Nearly fifteen hundred dollars. Probably more with penalties."

"I can give you that amount easily."

"It's too late for me to pay them. They're going to take my place. The only thing I can do is sell it to you and then you pay the taxes as the new owner."

"I can do that. Do you have the deed? If so, sign it over to me. Here's a buck."

Jedediah got up, walked along the bookcase, and stopped. I watched him pull a book, open it. He pulled out an envelope yellowed with age and handed it to me.

I carefully unfolded it. He owned 100 acres and the cabin. He signed it and handed it back to me. Tears welled up in his eyes and he turned his head to look away.

Someone banged on the cabin's door.

I went to the door. It was a sheriff.

"Jedediah Woods here?"

"Yes. Is there a problem?"

"Might be. Who are you?"

"I'm Adam and I own this place. Jedediah is my caretaker."

"You own this place? Since when?"

"Today. Just bought it and made arrangements for Jedediah to take care of the place for me when I'm away."

"You know there're back taxes due? I have an eviction notice."

"I am aware that there are taxes due. I will be in to pay them tomorrow. Unless of course, I can pay you right now."

"I don't know. I'll have to check with the judge about that."

"Well, why don't you pull up a stool and join us for some supper. We're about to eat," I said.

"I shouldn't but it sure does smell good," the sheriff said as he patted his belly.

"You have to eat somewhere so you might just as well join us," I said.

The sheriff was an agreeable man, probably fifty years old. While he was finishing off his second bowl of soup, it also became obvious that he didn't have a liking for the eviction. After the meal, Jedediah served up glasses of blackberry wine. The sheriff didn't seem in any hurry to leave.

"Let me call the judge and see what he says."

"You can call out from here? I've tried using my cell phone and can't get out," I said.

"The one in my car works just fine. It connects to the base."

"Could you do me a favor? I've been expecting a friend and he hasn't shown up. I was wondering if you could check and see if there have been any accidents between here and Williamsport in the last couple of days."

"No problem. Say that wine was good. You make that yourself, Jedediah?"

"Made it last summer after the berries ripened. Would you have another glass?"

"Don't mind if I do. I'll be right back."

The sheriff wasn't gone very long. The smile on his face told us the answer.

"The judge says you can pay me, I'll have to take it to the tax assessor's office, and you need to go to the court house and register the deed."

"Anything about my friend?"

"Nothing. No accidents, not even a fender bender."

I paid the sheriff and got a receipt. After he finished his wine, I walked him out to his car and asked him to check the city police to see if they had any reports on Running-water. They had no record of his arrest or of an accident.

I agreed to meet the sheriff tomorrow at the county court house. I also wanted to get a permit for a side arm. When I went back into the cabin, the look on Jedediah's face was extremely serious.

"We have some unfinished business," Jedediah said.
"What?"

"Meaningful and satisfaction. Or have you forgotten?"

"No, but before we get into that, I want you to know that as soon as Running-water arrives, I'll have him draw up a contract naming you as caretaker and giving you the right to live here until you die. Additionally, I'll pay you a monthly stipend to take care of essentials around here. Is that agreeable to you?"

"Yes. And does that give you meaning?" Jedediah said.

"Gives meaning to me? No. Does it have meaning for me? I suppose it does."

"And what meaning does it have for you?"

"That I've done the right thing. Did signing over your home to me give you a sense of satisfaction? Aren't you afraid I'll still kick you out and sell this place for a huge profit?"

"No, I've no concern about being kicked out. I feel satisfied with signing over my cabin and land to you. Somehow, I've known all along that I would do that. I did think it was supposed to be that mysterious friend of yours."

"And what does satisfaction mean to you?" I said.

"It means that I am content."

"And are you content with your life?"

"Yes. No, that's a lie. I'm not content at all. I'm lonely. Night after night, I sit here with my books and my thoughts, the more I read, and the more I think the more I realize it's all been for nothing. My life hasn't been worth a plugged nickel. You're too young to know what a sickening feeling that can be. Oh, I had a love and thought I had the world by its balls.

"What happened?"

"Well, one day I went to our secret place and she wasn't there. I continued to go at our agreed upon time for days, maybe weeks," Jedediah said.

"And you have no idea what happened."

"Yes. Several years later, I found out that my parents had paid her parents to get her out of town."

"Why?"

"They didn't think she was good enough for me. Didn't want me mixed up with an Indian and bringing in a bunch of half-breeds into the world."

"What a crock," I said.

" I never spoke to them again. When they died, I didn't go to their funerals. Why in the hell should I? They took away my life!"

" Since then, you've felt your life lacked meaning."

"Yes."

"Why did you move here?"

"I taught college for a short while thinking that would give me a sense of purpose. The hypocrisy of the faculty turned me off."

"Hypocrisy."

"They pretended to be interested in their students. Freshman girls became fair game for male faculty and the young males fair game for the female faculty. They claimed they were simply introducing them to life. Life, hell! It was to fulfill their own lust. Even the president of the college had been married and divorced several times, and was involved with a student."

"So, what happened?"

" I quit. Bought this land, cleared it, built the cabin, and have lived off the land since. My parents left me a small annuity. It ran out some time ago. I sold my truck to pay the taxes and then there was just not enough in social security to pay them and keep this place up. Even though I grew most of my own food, there were always a few staples I had to buy."

"Did you ever try to find her?"

"Yes. I spent every summer looking for her. Even hired a private detective. She had vanished from the face of the earth. Not a trace. Can you understand what it is to love someone so much that the entire world existed in that person? She was my hopes, desires, and ambitions. She created my sense of worth and dignity as a man.

"No! Maybe someday I will."

"And don't say it is better to have loved and not loved at all."

"That hadn't occurred to me. What I do see is that your love was self-destructive, self-effacing, and negative. You didn't think of your Self as valuable and therefore withdrew from society and from own personhood," I said.

"How can you say my love was self-effacing? She was my inspiration, my future, my—. "

"That's just the point, Jedediah. You completely obtruded your own Self, your personality, your very being. You lost sight of the fact that there had to have been something of value she saw in you. In essence, you became a non-person. You have allowed your bitterness to overshadow that aspect. She must have seen something wonderful and positive in you to love you. How can you dishonor that love by being a bitter recluse?"

"You sure don't mince your words do you, young fella? I guess I wasn't as smart as I thought I was because I didn't know how to mend a broken heart and then a broken life.

"'And now?" I said.

"What?"

"What about now? Are you going to continue to bury yourself in the dirt you farm? You have bent over so far physically it's almost as if you were willing yourself into the very earth you were plowing. And if you think that is not true just look at how straight you are right now. So what's it going to be, Jedediah? Die or get up and do something for yourself?"

"I suppose you feel real satisfied tearing up this old man's ass like that?"

"No need to get pissed at me, Jedediah. I'm simply telling it as I see it. If you want to get ticked, get mad at yourself."

"Humph."

We sat in silence for a good hour. Jedediah got up from the table and went to put a log on the fire.

"Don't do that! I'll do it," I said.

"So now you will tell me what to do?"

"Yeah. You work for me now, remember," I said as I put the log on the fire. "It's time to put the poultice on your back again and for you to have some more tea. Then in the morning, I'll try one more healing session with you. I don't think you'll be able to straighten up much more than you are, but I want to make sure you are healing."

After putting up a little fuss, he settled down.

"You're right you know," Jedediah said from his bunk.

"Right about what?"

"Everything. I am a bitter old man. I turned a beautiful love into an ugly hate filled life. Hate is ugly. Loneliness is not ugly but it not pleasant either. I mixed the two into one hell of a cocktail."

"Things will get better. Do you mind if I sit in your rocking chair? I'd like to read for a while."

"Help yourself. It's your place now."

"True, but it is your home," I said.

"So it is. So it is. Goodnight."

"Goodnight."

I banked the fire, lit the oil lamp, and took a copy of Alan Watts' *Does It Matter?* off the shelf. Watts was one of my favorites. I always found comfort in what he said.

It was nearly dawn when I finished the book. I felt better. I needed to be reminded that 'all existence is a single energy, and that this energy is one's own being.' [11] Watts made another point that hit home. He wrote that "the conceptual ego does not control this system [existence] any more than it controls the heart, but whereas the ego is your idea of yourself, the total energy system of the universe is what you are." [12] As part of that energy system, what I was feeling from Jedediah was not too far from my own personal feelings. That's why I was able to read him so clearly. Unfortunately, it's all too easy for an intuitive to read his own emotional Self into the being of another. That is something that I must try to avoid. Projection is not always the best way to help others.

"You going to sleep all day? There's plowing to be done." Jedediah said.

"What time is it?"

"Nearly nine o'clock. I see you read a good book. Learn
anything?"

"As a matter of fact, Jedediah, it does matter!"

"What matters?"

"Your feelings."

"How about some flapjacks for breakfast?

"Sounds good to me. And then we need to go to town. You know where the court house is?" I said.

"I don't see why I have to go. No need."

"Yes, there is. I need a character witness to buy a gun. Besides we need to pick out a few things for the farm."

"Well, if you insist. I haven't been into the county seat in years. I'll assume the court house still stands where it used to stand. Why do you want a gun?"

"Trouble follows me and I like to be prepared. You know how to shoot?"

"Of course."

"Good. There's a shotgun in the loft. I'll bring it down. You may have to use that."

"I don't understand."

"Hopefully you won't have to," I said.

Breakfast was quick. We headed for the county seat. A little over an hour later, we arrived in front of the court house. It was a large two-story sandstone building of the Federalist Style. Fourteen windows graced its front along with four large round pillars that reached to the top of the room.

The sheriff was waiting. We went into the clerk's office, registered the deed in my name, and then I asked the sheriff to join us at the local gun shop. I explained why I wanted to buy an automatic. And that I also wanted an extra clip. He agreed to issue the permit and wave the waiting period. I also bought several boxes of shells, loaded the 9mm, and strapped it on.

Two more stops and we had new truck and farm equipment for Jedediah and a load of what he called 'essentials'. The last stop was to have electrical power and telephone service installed at the farm. Satisfied with our day's accomplishments, we headed back to the cabin.

"There's a pretty good place to eat at the old hotel if you want to stop," Jedediah said after we had been on the road for over a half hour.

"I know it. Ate there before I came out to your place. I noticed a pay phone there. We'll stop. Maybe I can make contact with Dutch and find out about Running-water. It's not like him not to show up. Makes me uneasy."

I pulled the truck around to the back of the hotel and headed it out. Inside, as we sat down at a table, I spotted him. He was with two tough looking men; one seated by him on the outside, and the other across from him, effectively boxing him in so he couldn't make a run for it. Running-water looked like hell.

He looked up, saw me. I nodded and placed a finger to my lips.

"Jedediah, look in the mirror. Do you see that dark haired young man?"

"Yes."

"That's Running-water. He's in bad trouble. Walk by them and collapse? I'll rush to your aid and nail the bastards."

"Which one you want me to deck?"

"Just collapse. And stay on the floor."

Jedediah got up, walked a couple of feet, grabbed his chest, groaned, and then fell down on top of their table, not on the floor as I had instructed.

The two men struggled to get him off the table, and that was all the time I needed. I put a gun to one's head and Jedediah decked the other.

People scrambled everywhere once they saw my gun. Finally, we had two live people who had the answers to some of my questions. Forcing the two men to lay face down on the floor, we tied their hands to their feet, removed their wallets, side arms, and pulled their pants down as additional insurance.

"Oh, man. Am I ever glad to see you," Running-water said grabbing and hugging me.

"Not any more than I am to see you. What's this all about?"

" It's a very long story. I'm starved. These guys haven't fed me for several days. Can we get something to eat?"

"You bet. This is Jedediah Woods. He's been expecting you."

"Expecting me? How so."

"We'll talk about that later. Right now let's get you some food. Soup is about all you can handle by the looks of your face."

I watched as Running-water tried to spoon the soup into his barely open swollen lips.

By the time we finished our dinner, the sheriff walked in.

"Glad to see you, sheriff," I said, standing up to greet him.

"Looks like you were right. Trouble follows you. What's with the

two on the floor?"

A quick explanation from Running-water along with their unregistered guns was all the sheriff needed to cuff them and place them under arrest.

"There's an old barn down the road, let's just hang them," Jedediah said.

That gave me an idea. There might be a way to get some quick information out of those two bastards before they are taken to jail.

"Sheriff, may I see you outside for a few minutes?" I said.

Outside I convinced the sheriff to take the two men to the old barn Jedediah had mentioned and there do a little interrogation before hauling them off. Even though he was skeptical, he agreed to a pit stop before heading back to the county seat, and to the jail.

Once we got the men inside the old barn the sheriff produced a long rope that terrorized them. I pulled up an old box and sat on it directly in front of the two men who sat on the floor.

Leaning toward one of the men, I ran my finger down the bridge of his nose, blew into his eyes. He was under.

"Who hired you?" I asked.
"I don't know.

"How did you get your orders if you don't know who hired you?" I said.

"Telephone and recorded messages. Never met anybody."

"Tell me about the telephone and recorded messages. What did they say? Be very specific."

"We were paid five grand to kidnap a guy named Adam. He wasn't anywhere around so the voice on the phone told us to grab the guy we got. We were told where to go and once we had him to force him to lead us to this guy named Adam."

"The voice? Is it male or female?" I said.

"Don't know. It was disguised."

"How?"

"One of those things you put on a telephone to disguise your voice."

"How did you report back to this voice?"

"We had a number to call."

"You know that number?"

"Yes."

"Tell me the number."

As it was at Saint-Michaels, the number was no longer in service. The other man provided no additional information. The sheriff took them both out, put them in the back of his car, radioed for a back-up to meet him. Jedediah was very quiet as the three of us returned to the cabin. I noticed that he kept staring at Running-water.

Running-water was a physical mess. Jedediah suggested a soak and a glass of his corn. I helped him get his dirty, blood soaked clothes off. Deep cuts crisscrossed his back. He had been whipped.

"Those sons-of-bitches! They will pay for this, my friend. Believe me."

Jedediah brought out his horse liniment, but Running-water refused it.

"Let Adam take care of me."

We had to help him out of the tub. Jedediah insisted he lay down on his bunk. Running-water, in a great deal of pain, groaned as I helped him lay down on his stomach. I knelt down beside him, placed both hands on his back. I felt the terrible pain inflicted upon him, blow after blow. I also knew he never cried out.

My hands began to tingle, actually vibrate, and that was a new experience. Arcs of auric light began to flash from finger to finger as I moved my hands up and down his back. I stopped moving my hands and the light intensified. I wasn't sure what was happening. I just wanted to take my friend's pain away.

"My god, what's happening? There's fire flying all around your hands!" Jedediah said.

Before I could answer, Running-water raised his head and looked at me. "They kicked me in the balls so many times I don't think I have any left. I don't think I can ever have a son now," Running-water said as tears filled his eyes.

"Relax. Don't talk. All things are possible. Jedediah, some of your corn whiskey would be helpful about now. Pour it in the remaining tea and heat it up."

With some help, Running-water sat up and drank the tea. We wrapped a blanket around him and helped him to the table. Jedediah picked up his clothes and in doing so dropped a billfold. When he picked it up, it opened. I thought Jedediah had seen a ghost.

"Who's the woman in the photograph?" Jedediah said.

"My sister. Why do you ask?"

"She looks just like my Marrie."

"Your granddaughter?" Running-water said.

"No. The one and only love of my life. Tell me about your family."

"Jedediah, can you hold off on your questions until tomorrow? I know you've been waiting for Running-water to arrive but he's not in the best of shape right now and really needs to rest."

"In my excitement, I forgot. Of course, tomorrow or the day after will be fine. You best go back over there and lay down. Try to sleep. Adam and I will be right here."

Jedediah insisted he sit in his rocking chair and that Running-water have his bed. I brought my sleeping bag down from the loft, loaded the shotgun, as well as double checked my 9mm. I gave Jedediah the shotgun. He was to take the first watch. I would take the second.

Even though it was still early evening, I crawled into my sleeping bag and tried to go to sleep. I kept thinking about Daphne and how Jedediah reacted to her picture. Then there was the uncanny name of Marrie. Marrie Copa is the woman in Jedediah's past. They are Running-water's grandparents. That's the connection and Esaugetuh wanted me to bring them together. I'll be damned. It was Jesse and Mary, Al and Odora and now Jedediah and Marrie. I must remember to discuss this with Running-water. Sleep was out of the question so I got up and went over to Jedediah. He was awake.

"Jedediah, what would you say if I told you I know where Marrie is?" I whispered.

"You really know my Marrie?"

"I think so. Is it possible she had your child?"

"Yes. We were intimate. I never knew of any pregnancy but it makes sense to me now. My parents would have paid to get rid of the embarrassment. An illegitimate child, especially one from an Indian squaw as they called her, would not have been acceptable to them. It's her eyes that I see in the boy but his sister is a dead ringer for my Marrie. Who are they?"

"I believe they are your grandchildren. Would you like me to bring her here?"

"I'm old. She might not like what she sees."

"She is your age. She had some health problems but I think those are pretty much under control. She's still quite a woman."

" I suppose you took care of the health issues?"

"You could say I had a hand in it."

"There's no room here for her. You know I have no money to put her up at the hotel. Don't get me wrong. There's nothing I'd like more in this world but I'm not sure she would come. It's been a lot of years."

"Room is not an issue. Running-water and I can stay at the hotel. I think she'll come. Tomorrow we'll drive back to the hotel and call her. You can ask her yourself. My plane can bring her here in a matter of hours."

"We got company. You let me do the talking." Jedediah said.

"How do you know we got company?" I whispered.

"It got quiet out."

"Hello, the cabin."

"What do you want? It's late," Jedediah said

"Jedediah, it's Sheriff Logan. I want to talk to you and your friends if you don't mind. Sorry about the hour. It is important."

"Step back from the door," Jedediah said. Turning to me he continued, "You got that fancy light handy? If so aim it out that hole in the shutter."

It was the sheriff and he was alone. Jedediah unbolted the door and slowly opened it making sure the shotgun was at the ready.

"Sure am sorry about the hour. I need to know if your two friends are here. There's been a problem at the jail."

"What kind of problem, sheriff?" I said as I lit a lamp.

"Adam, those two men that kidnapped and beat your friend are both dead."

"How can that be?" Running-water said rousing himself from the bunk.

"My deputy heard a gurgling sound and went to check their cells. Both men were in their bunks, dead."

"What does the medical examiner say?" Running-water said.

"Don't know yet. There's the possibility they killed themselves but we don't know with what. A search of their persons was made during the booking process and they had nothing that could be used as a weapon," Sheriff Logan said.

"Did you see any marks on their neck, spots of blood, or a small hole?" I said.

"No. Well, actually I didn't look that close. How did you think to ask that?"

"Two men who tried to blow me up were found dead in their car not far from where my car was parked. Each man had a very small hole just under his right ear. Do you think you could get the coroner's report from Arizona?" I said.

"Sure. I can start that right now. I'll radio to my office and have them get started on that."

Turning to Running-water, the sheriff said, "Can you tell me anything else that might be helpful?"

"They grabbed me in my motel room. They were there waiting for me. I woke up in a warehouse of some kind. They wanted to know where Adam was. They found part of Jedediah's address in my computer bag. I had evidently not destroyed all of it after I copied it down. That's why we were at the hotel. They beat me for a week, kept food and water from me until we were at the hotel."

"And he was beaten most severely. They whipped him, stomped him, and broke several ribs. Had I known the extent of his injuries before we left the barn, they would have experienced pain as no living being has ever known," I said.

"Jedediah, you mind telling me how Adam happened to be here and just happened to buy your place?" Sheriff Logan said.

"Adam is the son of an old friend of mine. When I told him there was an eviction notice because of unpaid taxes, he bought the place. The rest you know."

"And Running-water's connection?"

"He is my grandson and Adam's attorney," Jedediah said.

"I didn't know you were ever married," Sheriff Logan said.

"I wasn't. His father, my son, was born out of wedlock."

"Hmm. I don't see a connection for all this other business. Adam, do you know why these men were after your friend?"

"Other than to get to me, none," I said.

"You're the target, why?"

"I don't know. We have tried to figure this out from all possible angles. I have inherited a very large fortune but there are no other heirs so I don't see why the effort to kill me. I have certain abilities that may or may not please some people. We haven't the slightest clue as to who is behind these attempts on our lives."

"You found nothing?" Jedediah said.

"Nothing. My office is checking driver licenses and I'm waiting on an autopsy. I suppose the State boys will come in and do an investigation. Anyway, we'll try to find out about their movements. There might be something coming in over the wire about the situation out in Arizona."

"Would it be helpful if you went out there, Sheriff Logan? Sometimes a direct contact gets more done," I said.

"Well I suppose it might, but the county can't afford to have me go traipsing all over the country."

"I'll fly you out there and back in my own plane. And you can escort Running-water's grandmother back. All expenses paid and I'll reimburse the county for you daily wages. What do you say?"

"Well, I don't see how the county supervisors could complain about that. I'll go home, pack a bag, stop by my office, and I'll be ready in a couple of hours."

"Good. Go to the airport at Williamsport, hanger four. My pilot will be waiting for you. His name is Dutch and the navigator's name is Brett. Both are former Navy SEALS and are well armed in the event you need extra fire power. Can you patch me through to this number on your car radio?" I handed him a card.

The sheriff was able to make the connection for me. I gave instruction for Dutch to fly the sheriff to Flagstaff, and then he and Brett were to drive him to Marrie's place.

I also placed a call to Marrie. When I told her Jedediah Woods wanted her to come for a visit, there was a very long pause.

"Marrie? Are you there? I said thinking her voice sounded strained."

"Yes. I didn't know he was alive. Adam, are you sure about this? Is it really Jedediah Woods?"

"Yes. No question about it. He's the father of your child. Will you fly out? If so, I'll have my pilot and our Sheriff Logan pick you up."

"Yes. Oh, my yes! I will. Oh, my! I just can't believe it. Can I talk to him?"

"Jedediah, she wants to talk to you., I said.

"Marrie is that you? Why didn't you —?"

"I wrote to you but you never answered my letters. Then one day I got this letter from your father saying you had killed yourself."

"Damn them! Will you come out here?"

"Yes! Oh, my yes! I just can't believe it. After all these years, Jedediah, it's really you."

"It's settled then," Jedediah said handing the mike back to me.

"Be ready, Marrie. Dutch will identify himself by telling you something only you know. Otherwise, don't let anyone in," I said.

"You still having troubles?" Marrie said.

"Yes. See you soon and remember, be careful."

"No use going back to bed. How about some breakfast? You too, Sheriff Logan." Jedediah said.

Jedediah outdid himself with the breakfast. He served up heaping stacks of pancakes, a dozen eggs, and coffee. Running-water was ravenous. He put up a fuss when I suggested he drink another cup of tea but he eventually drank it. He got fresh Echinacea leaves to eat.

"They were to help rebuild your immune system."

He excused himself and went outside. It was daylight now and the morning promised to be a good one.

"Adam, come here. I need you," Running-water yelled.

"What's the matter?" I said as I rushed out the cabin door.

"I'm urinating blood."

"Come back inside. I don't know if I can help you or not. All I can do is try."

"Good enough."

I went through the healing process again but felt Running-water should be hospitalized and that meant going back to Williamsport. Jedediah helped me get him in the truck. Sheriff Logan escorted us to the next county line. He radioed ahead for another escort. I had to drive slowly over the dirt road because of the ruts. Once I hit the paved road, I put the pedal down and we hauled ass.

Running-water insisted I stay with him during the doctor's examination. Surgery was necessary and he insisted I should be in the operating room with him. While the staff prepped Running-water, I called Dutch. Both he and Brett immediately came to the hospital. The surgery took a long time. The doctors repaired a kidney. In recovery, they told me it would be a couple of days before they would know if their work had been successful. I continued to stay with him in recovery.

Dutch introduced himself to Sheriff Logan and with my urging, they left for the airport. Sheriff Logan had met with the city police on duty just inside the recovery room. The guard noticed I was packing but said nothing. After what seemed an eternity, Running-water opened his eyes, reached out for my hand, and placed it on his abdomen.

"Do your thing, Adam. It's a good time." Running-water whispered.

Because I was tired and in an agitated state I wasn't sure how much good I would be able to do. Personal tension was high and it was difficult for me to calm myself. Running-water sensed this strain but misinterpreted it.

"Adam, I never told them anything. You've got to believe that."

"I know you didn't talk. I also know you never cried out nor let them know how much pain they were inflicting on you. I am distressed because you had to suffer. I should have been the one they got, not you. I promise you this, I will find who is responsible for all of this, and they will experience an unimaginable terror. Justice has been denied. We've been cheated out of knowing who's behind all of this. That was then and this is now. And now, my friend it's time we declared all-out war. Now I must ask you to remain quiet and to steady your breathing as much as possible. Clear your thoughts about anything negative. I have to do the same."

I started to place my hands on Running-water but I felt a sudden repulsion. I tried again and again but my hands were repelled. My hands began to hover about two inches above his body. Having a life of their own, they slowly moved over the full length of Running-water's body, stopping at the area of surgery, lingering there as if to read what had happened. I had only a vague sense of what was happening. It was like watching a surrealistic slow moving picture. Time slowed and then stopped! It was unlike any of my previous healing experiences. I wasn't controlling anything yet I was aware of being present more as an observer than as participator.

As I stood there with my hands stretched out over Running-water, a glow began to emanate from his body. As it slowly rose up and took shape, I knew I was looking at his soul.

"No! No!" I cried out. "Not now!"

The startled guard rushed to the bed. I collapsed sobbing. He helped me to a chair. I don't know how long I sat there devoid of all feeling, numb to all existence, an automaton incapable of any movement. For the first time in my life, I felt totally alone.

"Hey, you finished doing your thing yet?"

"Running-water? My god, I thought you had died!" I said grabbing and hugging him.

"What?"

"I saw your soul leave your body. I was sure you had died." I said as I pushed the call button.

A nurse came in. I asked her to check Running-water. She said everything was fine except I looked terrible. She pinched my ass as she left. And that tickled Running-water because he burst out laughing even though it must have hurt. An orderly wheeled in a cot for me to sleep on. I dozed on and off and was aware of a change of the guard. Also registering was the fact that the guard we had didn't know the relief man and that set up red flags. I reached under my pillow and readied my gun. He moved toward my cot, leaned over, and put a gun to my head. The sound of the shot brought the nurses running to our room. They turned on the lights and saw a man thrashing around on the floor.

"Call the security and the police. This man tried to kill me. He'll need medical attention as well."

"What the hell. Another one?" Running-water said. "Man they sure do want you dead."

Security and a medical team were in the room within minutes. The police arrived very shortly after that. The hit man was not one of their officers and this caused them concern as to what happened to the officer that was supposed to come on duty.

"Man, you shot this guy's balls of," said an intern.

"He's lucky. I could have killed him."

As intern and nurses lifted him onto a gurney I said, "Tell your friends I've declared war and I'm not through with you yet, not until you know total terror."

I walked around the gurney and passed my hands over his face and eyes. Suddenly he began screaming and fighting the air with his hands.

"Put it out. My god, I'm on fire. Please, I beg you, put it out. I can't stand it."

"Better get him to O.R.; he's losing it," said the intern.

"Wonder why he thought he was on fire?" said a nurse.

"The world is full of weirdoes if you ask me?" said another nurse.

"Yeah, ain't it the truth," said another as they wheeled my would- be assassin away.

"How do they know where we are?" Running-water said.

"I don't know. I'm beginning to think we are personally bugged."

"Adam."

"What?"

"You could be right. Could we or one of us have had an implant of some kind?"

"One way to find out. We'll have a CAT-scan. You doing okay?"

"Yeah."

"Good. Try to get some rest."

"You, too."

I stepped into the hallway and continued to talk with the police officers. There was a natural concern about their missing officer. Two are now at Running-water's room, one inside and one outside. Their professionalism impressed me. I went to the nurses' station and asked them to have the chief of staff see me as soon as he arrived.

As it turned out, the chief of staff was Dr. Ann Milford, an amiable lady in her fifties. She was very solicitous and arranged for Running-water and me to have body scans. By eleven o'clock, the technician had found no implants. The disappointment showed. It would have been an answer to how we were being tracked. Maybe it's the plane itself. Flight plans provide destination and time of arrival as well as departure. I wondered who's calling the flight services and giving them the N number of my plane? I asked one of the officers to check and see if someone had made an inquiry last night and if he could find out who it was. I went back into the room to discuss this with Running-water and found him fully dressed and ready to leave.

"Where do you think you are going?" I said.

"We are going back to the cabin," Running-water replied.

"I don't think you should be going anywhere."

"Look, all they are doing here is monitoring me. I can come back to have the stitches removed."

"They need to see if that kidney is functioning the way it's supposed to and they can't do that back at the cabin. You are staying put."

"I urinated just fine with no sign of any blood. The nurse took her time checking. The same one that pinched your butt. Besides, you did your thing and I'm healing just fine."

"Well, I can see you are well enough for certain things," I said laughing.

An officer came into the room and told us that there had been an inquiry about the plane. Running-water suggested we notify Dutch and have him take extra precautions.

"It's something, you know. After all of the years believing I had no living grandparents, I suddenly have them, a grandfather and a grandmother, one white and one Apache. Guess that makes me a half-breed. All along I thought I was a fine full-blooded Apache specimen," Running-water said.

"Has the fact that your grandfather is white diminished who you are? Has it changed the man I know as Running-water, the man I know as my friend? Your ancestry or your color does not make you a man. What's inside does. I see a man of extraordinary courage and bravery, a man anyone would be proud to call brother. And I am very proud of you, my brother."

"You're right, Adam. I am that I am."

"And so you are."

While the paper work progressed for Running-water's release from the hospital, I called the airport and asked them to relay a message to Dutch. Whoever is behind all of this may assume I'm on the plane and may be waiting.

As I was hanging up, one of the detectives stopped and told me that the man who attempted to kill me was from New York but that didn't mean anything to me.

"You know, Adam, when Marrie gets here she and Jedediah will want to be alone. A romantic evening is really not possible with two other guys in that small cabin. It might be a good time for us to go and check on your home. It's not that far a drive from here is it?"

"I don't have a home. We can leave tomorrow for my parents' place. Maybe it is just as well that you haven't had time to contact my parents' attorney. I think I still have a key to their house. We can stay there. You sure you are up to a four hour drive?"

"No problem. Can we pick up my gear of the motel?"

CHAPTER 9 - A SHORT STAY

No man is born unto himself alone;
Who lives unto himself, he lives to none
Francis Quarles

After picking up Running-Water's gear, we headed to Jedediah's. When we arrived, he was in the fields plowing with his new tractor. Jedediah was greatly relieved to see Running-water and disappointed that we would not be staying. I packed up my stuff, loaded the truck, and wished Jedediah much happiness. He made us promise to come back.

I had some misgiving about going to where my parents lived. In addition to their deaths, and the business with their attorney, there was Jacqueline. I didn't really want to see her, meet her husband, or know anything about them. Any feelings I once had have long gone and it is better not to renew old acquaintances. It would be necessary to call on her parents. I dreaded the long explanation they would expect.

The house itself would bring back a few memories; of course, nothing from early childhood since my parents moved there after I had graduated from high school. I spent that first summer there and then had gone off to the university. My visits were infrequent during those years. Then I moved back and commuted into New York where I had worked as a free-lance researcher. I had convinced a magazine editor that her readers would be interested in shamanism and that began my search for Esaugetuh. Years later, a million miles, and several lives after that, here I am on my way back to where I used to live.

Anyway, here we are snaking our way over two-lane roads headed southeast. Running-water has been sleeping much of the time. He moaned and seemed to be in dream time. Perhaps I can heal his body but I don't think my abilities go as far as removing the memories of the ugliness that befell him. At our first stop, I'll try another healing session. It still concerns me that he left the hospital so soon after major, major surgery. I wonder if there is a shaman located in the Poconos. There used to be many tribes throughout that area. Perhaps Running-water's sister could get that information for me. I pulled into a self-service, hit the head, and then began tanking gas. Running-water woke up and went to the head to relieve himself. He knew by the look on my face that I was going to ask him about blood.

"Normal," he said.

"You hungry?" I said.

"Yeah. I could eat. They have hot food?"

We went in, picked up some fried chicken, a couple of salads, and two pops. After we finished eating, I suggested another healing session. This time instead of working on his back, I simply placed a hand on each side of the back of his neck. The heat built quickly. "Let me know if the heat gets too much."

"It feels great."

"Good. I want this session to last fifteen minutes. So no squirming around. You got it?"

"Yeah, yeah."

I sensed that he was really healing and felt no inflammation. Only a full body scan would tell me the whole story. That would have to wait until we reached our destination. Hyde Park was another couple of hours away.

"You know, Adam, what we need instead of this truck is one of those motor homes. Can we rent one of those?"

"We'll check into it. It sure would beat sleeping on the ground or on the floor at Jedediah's."

"Did you really buy his place for just a buck? What are you going to do with it?"

"Jedediah had wanted to give it to you. I think deep down he knew that you were his grandson but was afraid to hope. That's why he kept asking me about the person that was supposed to be with me. It's yours and as long as Jedediah and Marrie are alive and want to live there they are to have it."

You're serious about giving me that property?"

"Yes."

"But why? You bought it, paid the back taxes on it. You bought the new truck, tractor, and other equipment. You are the one having it modernized. Haven't you ever heard that 'charity' begins at home?"

"Sure, but what does that mean?" I said.

"That you look out for yourself."

"Okay, but how do you do that?"

"Think of yourself first," Running-water said.

"Well, the notion of "charity begins at home" has a number of implications for the Self," I said.

"Such as?"

First, I think is the acceptance of who and what you are. Don't waste your effort being self-critical and berating yourself and your value as a human being."

"Great! Just great. Doing that is a hell of a lot easier said than done. I still don't get the connection you are drawing to charity."

"Well, if you beat yourself up all the time where's the charity in that? You have to be honest when it comes to your strengths and weaknesses. Being honest and truthful about your desires, ambitions, or goals takes into account those strengths and weaknesses as well. Understanding those eliminates the need to beat yourself up. Self-deprivation is an illusion. It doesn't bring you peace or happiness."

"Okay, I'll go along with that for now. So, what's the bottom line?" Running-water said.

"If you have no charity toward yourself how can you show charity toward others?"

"That's sure a long explanation of why you gave me the cabin. Why did you really give it to me?" Running-water said.

"Because it is right, because you are my friend, or because we are Brothers. Take your pick. It's yours and that's that."

"Man, I can't believe you are for real."

"Stop jumping around. And be quiet."

"Nag, nag."

The session finished, we headed northeast. I didn't plan to stay overnight on the road. Burgers and fries became our supper. A couple of pit stops later and we were in Hyde Park.

My parents' house was a Victorian with the traditional tower on the front corner of the house. It had four bed rooms, three full baths, a family room, a formal living room, a dining room, a library-music room, two fireplaces, and an attached garage for three cars.

My key wouldn't fit the lock on the back door. I wonder why my parents changed the lock. I smashed a window, reached in, and unlocked the door.

I got the lights on and began a systematic check of the house. The remains of cigar smoke still lingered in the library. Running-water noticed it also. The search of the house found no one. We brought in our gear and stashed it in the hallway. I found a piece of plywood and put that up over the broken window. Running-water opened the refrigerator to put in some cans of pop.

"Looks like someone was expecting us. Three bottles of champagne. No food, though."

"That's odd. Why would the refrigerator be running all this time? Wonder if the freezer is still going and what'll be in that?" I said.

We didn't have to time investigate because the doorbell rang and there was a pounding on the front door. I strapped on my gun and then went to the door.

"Come out with your hands behind your head."

"On whose orders?"

"Police."

I opened the door slightly, leaving the guard chain fastened.

"Adam, is that really you? My god, everyone around here thought you were dead. It's Pete. Pete Ross. You remember me?"

"I'll be damned. Come on in. How've you been?"

"Fine. The question is where have you been? You didn't even come to your folks' funeral."

"It's a long story. Do you know what's been going on here? The lock's been changed and I know someone was in here and left not too long before we arrived."

"Well, I can say I bet Jacqueline will be glad you 're back. Word has it that she's not very happy that her husband has a new interest."

"Does he smoke cigars?"

"Yeah. Guess you know who's been here. Rumor has it that he's been using this as his love nest. Some say she even caught them in the act. "

"I want him arrested for trespassing."

"Well I don't know about that, his dad's and him being lawyers."

"I don't care if he's the governor. He has no right to be in my house. I am the executor of my parents' will and their sole heir. I want this place gone over for finger prints, and I want a warrant issued for his arrest. This is my attorney. His name is Paul."

"Better do as Adam wants. He can get real ugly."

"Pete, do you know of any effort to locate me when my folks died? Do you know anything about their deaths?"

"They were killed in a one car accident. The state police said it was alcohol related. I don't believe there was any serious effort to locate you. There was a statement in the news item about the accident that your whereabouts were unknown."

"Was an autopsy made?"

"I don't know, but I sure can find out if you want."

"Yes, do that for me. And Pete, keep it mum," I said.

"No problem. You think something is fishy?" Pete said.

"Yes. My father was not a heavy drinker. He took a drink in the evening, shot of whiskey, and no chaser. My mother never drank."

"I never saw him at any of the local bars. By the way, the neighbors called and said they heard glass being broken and saw a truck in the back. They'll want to know what's going on. I'll have to stop over there. You want me to tell them you have come home?"

"Tell them whatever you think is necessary. You sure took a chance coming up on the porch alone." I said.

"I'm not alone; two other officers are with me. One's out back and the other is just outside the door. You always pack a gun?" Pete said.

"These days I do. And yes, I know how to use it. I have a permit to carry from Pennsylvania."

"Not much good here, even if we do have a reciprocal agreement. If you plan on going about with that on you, you better register. I'll be in touch with you, Adam. Nice to have you back. You want me to let Jacqueline know?"

"No. It's better to let the past be the past. I'm sorry she has been having a rough time. She doesn't deserve that. Say, you were always sweet on her. You still carrying the torch?"

Pete's face turned red and like an embarrassed teenager, he shuffled his feet "Don't worry, I'm no competition. And I'll still keep your secret. Have you ever told her how you feel?"

"I can't do that. She's married. Besides, why'd she want a cop?"

"You never know until you ask."

"Yeah, yeah. Take care, Adam. I'll be in touch."

"So you and this Jacqueline were a number?" Running-water said.

"It seems like a thousand years ago. We were never officially engaged, just an agreement to get engaged. It was more our parents' idea and we went along with it. Leaving and going on my search for Esaugetuh was the right thing to do."

"By the way, am I now to use my Christian name? I noticed you introduced me as Paul," Running-water said.

"It just seemed natural under the circumstance. I will call you by whichever name you prefer. I didn't mean to offend you."

"No problem. Just wondered."

The doorbell rang. Two forensic specialists had arrived. They would go over the entire house. They asked us where we had been in the house, took our fingerprints and footprints.

While they were busy doing their job, the phone rang. For a moment, I couldn't remember where it was. Finally, I remembered and went to the library, found the phone, looked at it. Jonathan Randolph, my parents' attorney, was calling.

"This is Jonathan Randolph. Why in the hell didn't you say you were coming back and moving in? You should have let me know."

"Why? What's the big deal? It's my house."

"Well, that's just the point. There's a claim against the property."

"I don't know anything about a claim. My attorney, Paul Dakota will be in touch with you. He's here in town with me. Maybe in a few days."

I hung up.

Every sensor in my body was going off. I also knew that it was a good idea to listen to my inner voice. Jonathan Randolph was not to be trusted. I supposed one of the neighbors called him and told him someone was in the house.

"Adam." It was Running-water. "I'm not offended by your calling me by my Christian name. It's just that I—."

"What? Okay, no problem. That was Jonathan Randolph, my parents' attorney. I told him you would be in touch in a few days. See what you can find out. Whatever you do, Running-water, do not turn your back on this one or let him distract you. I have off the wall negative vibrations about him. I even felt that way when I talked to him from Miami."

"Not to worry. I see there's a computer here. I can connect with my laptop and do some poking around."

I went down the hall to the family room and started to lay down on a couch.

"Sir, the forensic team is still working this area," a young woman said.

"Sorry."

I decided to check out the freezer that was in the basement. It was full of meats, frozen vegetables, pies, and bread. There was enough food to last a couple of months. I then checked the walk-in pantry. All kinds of canned goods and several bottles of my father's favorite whiskey lined the shelves.

I picked up one to take up stairs with me and inadvertently looked at the seal. It had been broken.

I thought that strange since the bottle was full. I checked the other bottles and they all had broken seals. I hunted around for a box in which to put the half dozen bottles.

Upstairs, I looked for the forensics specialist. Found one still in the library.

"I have six bottles of whiskey that have their seals broken. Can you analyze the content of each to see if something else is in the bottles? Any sign of a drug that would induce sleepiness, especially if it would double the impact when combined with the alcohol."

I was careful to point out the one bottle I had really handled and the rest I had picked up near the bottom of each bottle because I wanted them dusted for prints.

They found several sets of prints throughout the house. They would look for a match. They found semen on the couch in the library as well as in one of the bedrooms. Strands of blond hair came from one of the bathrooms. According to the forensic team, they had a good sample. It would take a couple of days to get a report.

Pete Ross came back to the house. There had been no autopsy on my parents. I asked him who was sitting as judge these days. Judge Hackett was still on the bench. I started to call him but thought to check the phone for a bug. Sure enough, I found one.

"I'll be damned. Adam, what's going on here? You hold on a minute. Let me get some other people in here," Pete said.

It wasn't long before another team arrived and began going over the house for other electronic bugs.

"This is really impressive, Adam. These guys really know their business, Running-water said.

"Adam, we've found two other phones bugged and bugs in the lamps of the library but we can't find the recorder," Pete said.

"You think it's being transmitted somewhere else?" Running-water said.

"No. This equipment is not that sophisticated," Pete said.

"Hey, Pete, come to take a look at this. I think the recorder's been found," said one of the policemen.

The recorder was in a drawer of a built-in out in the garage. We listened to our conversation as well as earlier conversations between Running-water and myself, and the call from Jonathan Randolph.

"Strange, there is no other talk or noise on the tape," I said.

"Play it again. I think I heard something," Running-water said.

The tape was played again at a slower speed.

"There, that sounds like a door closing," Running-water said.

"Guess, that rules out Jacqueline as the person responsible for all the bugs as a means of collecting evidence against her errant husband," Pete said.

I noticed the sign of relief as Pete continued, "That leaves one of the two Randolphs, or both of them as possible culprits. I think the place is clean. If you want to use the phone go ahead."

"Thanks. I want to call Judge Hackett. By the way, you sure pull a lot of weight to get all of these people out here. What's your position on the force?"

"I'm the chief."

"Congratulations. That's great! No wonder you can get things done." I said. "Maybe you should be the one to call Judge Hackett. Get an order to have my parents' bodies exhumed. Also, get a warrant for young Randolph's arrest. Let's get the whole thing out in the open."

"Can do. You'll have to sign an agreement to have their bodies exhumed."

"You got it. Running-water, you come up with anything on the Randolphs?"

"Some interesting things came up. I heard you say you were calling a judge. You may want to ask him to sign a court order for the release of Randolph's bank records. There's been a lot of money moved around."

"Hmm. Maybe it would be better if you paid Mr. Randolph a visit right now That is, if you feel up to it," I said.

"No problem. By the way, do you have a copy of your parents' will?"

"No, but I know where it's kept. It's in the safe."

"I'm sure whoever has been here and whoever has been behind this has gone through that safe by now," Running-water said.

"Nope. It's hidden. Let's go check it out."

We went upstairs and into one of the bathrooms. There, I turned off the water so the tank wouldn't refill, flushed the toilet, and then pushed on the back of the tank forcing it to slide down. Behind it was a wall safe. The team that was doing the dusting for prints did a dusting on the safe. I then opened it. Several envelopes were inside. I gave them all to Running-water. I closed the safe and returned everything back to the way it was. Back downstairs, we opened some of the envelopes. One contained the will. It was as I had said; I was the executor and only heir. Other envelopes contained copies of the deed, insurance policies, including a five million dollar policy with the estate named as the chief beneficiary. A sub clause caught Running-water's attention.

"Here it is, Adam. The answer."

"What? What answer?"

"The reason you have had all these attempts on your life. In the event there is no living heir, the estate goes to Randolph and Randolph Law Firm. It seems to me that there is no connection to the disappearance of Esaugetuh, the Vegas duffle bag, and the people on the list. You were targeted in order to get your parents' estate. I wonder if we can establish that Randolph was on the island prior to or during the time of the attack on Saint-Michaels. Do you suppose he has a recorded message on one of his phones that says the 'number is no longer in service?' Don't we have an area code from the last attempt?"

"Not only do I have the area code, I also have the number. Same area code as here. Let's see what happens?" I said as I dialed the number.

We got the 'no longer in service message' but we heard the familiar click as the line switched to a message machine.

"I don't think you better go over to Randolph's alone. Pete, what do you suggest?" I said.

"At this point, you have motivation but no specific concrete evidence. I wouldn't confront Randolph just yet."

"I'd sure like to smoke the bastard out," I said.

"Have your attorney set up an appointment as you have said you would. Keep it strictly related to the business of settling the estate. In the meantime, I can find out about the telephone number."

"I suppose you're right. I'm just not sure, " I said.

" I'm also positive as soon as I request search warrants and the order to exhume your parents' bodies, it will be all over town and in the papers. Fact is, I'd like to sit on that until I get the forensic reports."

"He's right, Adam. We should pull back. That'll give me time to see if I can connect any of the men who made attempts on your life to the money moved around in the Randolph accounts," Running-water said.

"Correction. Our lives," I said.

"You two plan on staying here?" Pete said.

"Sure. Any reason why we shouldn't?" I said.

"Well, with all the attempts on your lives, I'd say it might be a good idea to stay somewhere else. You can stay at my place."

"Okay. Let's put the bugs back. Running-water, why don't you call Mr. Randolph and set up an appointment and in passing let him know we'll be staying elsewhere. Say in the city."

The bugs were replaced along with the tapes and the recorder. Running-water made his call. He didn't have to indicate we were not staying at my parents' house because Randolph asked. We turned off the lights, locked up, and drove our truck to Pete's condo. One of us would have to make use of the sleeping bag and since it was mine, I made the choice. As was our custom, one of us took the first watch. Running-water took that. The night remained uneventful and the dawn brought no new threats.

The appointment with Jonathan Randolph was not until one o'clock. He had agreed to meet at a restaurant for lunch. In the meantime, I had decided it would be a good idea to change the location of the meeting. Running-water called Randolph about an hour before we were to meet and changed the location claiming he couldn't get reservations. Reluctantly, Randolph agreed to the change. I would go with Running-water. Pete would have his people in place at the restaurant.

Running-water and I waited in the parking lot. Once we saw Randolph go into the restaurant, we would then go in. It also added a little insurance against a possible car bomb. We had had enough of those.

Randolph arrived in a Mercedes convertible His finely tailored dark blue suit, Florida tan, and a mop of white hair made him an immediate stand-out. I detected no sense of uneasiness as he strolled into the restaurant.

"Man, that guy sure doesn't act like he's coming to a meeting that will destroy him," Running-water said. "Makes me very suspicious."

"I always say, listen to your inner warnings. Generally, there's a good reason you have them."

Inside, we found Randolph seated at a table and joined him. He was politely cool as he again offered his condolences. Everything moved right along without any problems until Running-water told Randolph that the insurance claim had been made.

"Since it is such a large amount, the insurance company is insisting of a routine investigation to the cause of Adam's parents' deaths.

"You notified the insurance company?" His tan face flushed with anger, Randolph continued, "How dare you do that without first consulting me!"

"Excuse me! My client doesn't need your permission to do anything. This meeting was just a courtesy, Mr. Randolph. I can see that you did not receive it as that. We have a meeting with Judge Hackett within the hour to sign papers to have my client's parents' bodies exhumed. Apparently, there wasn't an autopsy and the insurance company wants one."

I thought Randolph was going to pass out. The veins in his neck bulged just above his collar line. It amazed me that he regained his composure so quickly.

"I don't see the need for an autopsy. It was common knowledge that your father liked his booze. He always kept several bottles shelved in the basement. The insurance company won't pay a dime if they read the state patrol's report on the accident and I have managed to get the only copy of the original report. I tried to protect you, Adam, and this is the thanks I get. You bring in a fancy lawyer from god knows where and sit there and let him insult me." Randolph said.

"There's no need to feel insulted. You know perfectly well that as the executor of his parent's estate, my client is simply following standard procedures," Running-water said.

"I'd forgotten about the whiskey. I can't even remember the name of the brand he used to like," I said.

"He drank a hundred proof Canadian. Always had his name on the label. Well, you two had better run along. Judge Hackett doesn't like to be kept waiting."

"Man, we sure were dismissed, like a couple of little kids. That guy is one tough customer," Running-water said as we left the restaurant.

"I warned you, you remember, " I said, heading to our car.

Pete was there waiting for us.

He had a report back from the forensic lab with positive identification on two sets of prints; one belonging to Randolph junior and another to his father, Jonathan's prints were on the liquor bottles. Additionally, all of the bottles had enough drugs in them to cause an intensified reaction to the liquor.

"Anything on the telephone numbers?" I said.

"Oh, yeah. They belong to the senior Randolph. We have enough evidence to go for an arrest. The judge granted the search warrants. We're set to go."

"There's Randolph, just leaving the restaurant," Running-water said. "Guess he doesn't see us."

We watched as Randolph got into his car.

"You going over there and serve the warrants?" I said.

A gunshot shattered the quiet.

We ran to Randolph's car. He was already in his death throws. He had placed the bullet well. There was an envelope in one hand and a thirty-eight in the other. Pete called in for an ambulance and crime scene investigators.

"You two have an appointment with the judge. Judge Hackett doesn't like to be kept waiting. You better get going," Pete said.

"Yeah, you're right. Catch you later," I said.

Judge Hackett was a distinguished looking gentleman in his early sixties. Bushy eyebrows accentuated his dark brown eyes. He signed the order to exhume my parents, ordered an autopsy, and directed us to the clerk's office.

Running-water completed the necessary paperwork and registered me as the new owner of the house. I didn't want the house nor anything of its furnishings. There might be some photos but other than that, I had no interest in keeping it. I wanted it sold including the furniture and my mother's car.

Our next stop was at a realtor who jumped at the chance to sell the old house. She said we should put a price tag on it for eight hundred thousand. She also knew an auctioneer and would have him meet us at the house for an appraisal. It would take several days to do an inventory; the coroner's inquest also would take several days, and it might take several months for the insurance company to settle.

" Running-water, I don't want to stick around for any of this. Can we simply set up an account and have everything put in that and then have a final rendering?"

"No problem. We can use any bank you want. You have an account here?"

"Yes. We can use the one that manages my trust fund."

"Trust fund?"

"Yeah, my grandfather left me enough money to assure I would be financially independent."

"Very nice."

The bank business didn't take long. Back at Pete's condo, Running-water took a much needed nap. He hadn't completely healed from the terrible beating he had taken. It concerned me that he was so pale and lacking in energy.

While he napped, I called Dutch to confirm his return with Marrie and that he and Brett had delivered her safely to Jedediah.

Dutch had Sheriff Logan's report on the death of the two men parked outside of Marrie's apartment.

"What do you mean they were killed with something injected into their brains?" I said.

"You're not going to believe this. Logan said it was ice.

"Ice?"

"Yes, ice. It was injected into the brain under tremendous pressure," Dutch said.

"I know there was a hole behind their right ear. The report indicates what caused that hole?"

"The sheriff said the holes appeared to have been made by a 22 riffle. And that means the bullets were made of ice."

"Wouldn't there have been spent casings around if bullets were used? I said.

"I don't know, you'll have to ask somebody who's into ballistics."

"I can ask Pete? He just walked in."

"Who's Pete?"

"The chief of police. I'll talk to you later."

"Ask me what?" Pete said.

I gave him a quick explanation, but he didn't know of any specific weapon.

"I think the Russians developed an ice bullet used for assassination, but I'm not sure. I can check NYPD if you like.

"Let that ride for now. What did you find at Randolph's office?"

"When I went to serve the warrant at Randolph and Randolph Law Offices, I found Randolph's son dead. He apparently killed himself. As soon as forensic is finished, we'll box up most of the stuff in their office. The letter the old man had in his hand was a full confession detailing the murder of your parents. Evidently, he made some wrong investments and borrowed heavily to cover the loss. The people he borrowed from were not the type to allow a default when the loan came due. Evidently, he used some of their resources to try and kill you."

"Do you think I'm still a target?"

"Can't say for sure. I'd think they might back off as soon as they find out that both of the Randolphs are dead and the only way for them to collect on the loan is to sue the estate. I don't think they'll get much." Pete said.

"How is Jacqueline taking all of this?"

" She expressed concern for her mother-in-law."

"You know it might be a good idea if you too spent some time over there with her. She'll need a friend."

Pete's face turned red at my suggestion. He shuffled his feet like a typical teenager on his first date.

"Will it be necessary for us to remain here?" I said.

"I don't think so. I can't see any reason for a Grand Jury to request your appearance, however, if you are required to be here, how can I reach you?"

"Use my cell phone number. Thanks for all your help, Pete. By the way, if you and Jacqueline get it together, I own a great place on an island. Perfect for a secluded honeymoon. It's yours to use anytime."

"I got your number. And thanks for the offer. I might just take you up on that."

"As soon as Running-water is up, we'll hit the road."

CHAPTER 10 - ON THE ROAD AGAIN

If you bring forth what is within you, what you bring forth will save you. If you do not bring forth what is within you, what you do not bring forth will destroy you.

Jesus Christ

Running-water came out from his nap. He had mentioned getting a motor home to travel in and the idea had a certain appeal. We stopped at a dealer, found one we both liked and bought it. It had a 500 horsepower engine with six speed electric transmission, one monster bedroom, and two smaller bedrooms, two full showers, and a complete kitchen. He had convinced me to keep my mother's Mercedes convertible instead of keeping the truck to tow

Three names remain on our list, two men, and one woman. Running-water has not run a check on them. He is ill-at-ease. If he's not pacing up and down, he's trying to sleep. It's not a restful sleep because he frequently moans. I feel the cause of this is the trauma his body suffered from the brutal beating he received.

I also feel that my ability to heal him, to wash away his pain, and to ease his spirit is limited. This healing business is too new to me. I sure wish Esaugetuh was here; he would know what to do. On two occasions, I mentioned it might be a good idea to go back to the hospital for a checkup. Each time I did, Running-water became agitated refusing to discuss it further.

We had been on the road for several hours and it surprised me that we had actually stopped moving.

Daylight was just making her appearance. I looked around and realized I was in the parking lot of the hospital at Williamsport.

"I'll be damned. I sure don't remember heading back here," I mumbled.

I eased out from behind the steering wheel and checked on Running-water. He was asleep. Being careful not to wake him, I slipped out of the motor home and went into Admissions. As luck would have it, the doctor who had operated on Running-water was on duty. After a brief explanation and an expression of my concerns, the doctor agreed to check on Running-water.

As we entered the motor home, we both heard him moaning, and saw him lying in a pool of blood, eyes closed, and barely conscious. When I bent down, he opened his eyes and I saw death.

Gently I took his ashen face into my hands. I wasn't sure what I was doing but in the back of my head was the story of Christ and the blind and dumb man. I couldn't remember the word or words Christ spoke, but I knew the intent.

My hot hands caused beads of perspiration to form around his brow. Even as the orderlies placed him on a gurney, I managed to keep my hands in place. By the time, we were in the hospital I felt like the proverbial wet rag. My body seemed to collapse. I eased my way down to the floor and leaned back against the wall. My hands are swollen and are bright orange red.

"You okay, sir?"

"I'll be fine," I said, accepting a glass of water offered to me by the orderly.

Whatever transpires now must come from Running-water. I know of nothing more to do. I finished the glass of water, got up, went into the waiting room, and slumped down in a chair.

Talk about hell on earth! It surely must be a hospital waiting room. Time drags slower than any imagined snail. Television is an annoyance, coffee tastes like it had a hangover, and hushed conversations become irritants. Calls over the public address system force their way into the creeping numbness that begins to engulf what's left of rational processes.

Fifteen people have died since my quest, including my parents; Esaugetuh is nowhere to be found, and now the only friend I have is in a desperate battle for his life. If he dies—the thought struck deep and I shuddered at its new presence, I will be totally alone. The prospect of being totally alone had never occurred to me before.

Daphne, Running-water's sister, would be alone. No! There are Jedediah and Marrie for her.

Of course, Marrie. Why hadn't I thought of this before? She may know of a shaman, a ritual, something that will help Running-water. Damn. I left the number out in the motor home.

Luck was with me, I found the number and the telephone line had been run to the cabin.

Jedediah answered. He said he and Marrie would come to the hospital immediately. The distress in his voice deepened my own concern.

Dr. Redmond was waiting for me when I returned to the hospital.

"He's in critical condition," she said. "Besides the loss of a great deal of blood, one kidney has stopped functioning and the other is in a near failure mode."

"What about a kidney transplant?" I said.

"We don't have a donor and it may take too long to find one. Even then it may be too late."

"What about me?"

"It's a long shot and risky. You sure you want to go through—."

"Of course. Let's get it going."

"There are papers you have to sign, blood work to be done. Let me get things set up."

"Whatever it takes to keep Running-water alive, do it. If you need specialists, just let me know. I have a jet at the airport and we'll get them here."

"Fine. I'll be back as soon as possible. If you want, you can wait with your friend. By the way, does he have another name besides Running-water?"

"Paul, Paul Dakota."

I went to Running-water's room and sat down beside his bed. His closed eyes seemed puffy and his breathing shallow.

I wonder where Esaugetuh is and why he has not communicated with me since we left Saint-Michaels'. It sure would be a good time for some advice. Whatever powers I seem to have as a healer aren't strong enough to help my friend.

I was so absorbed in my own thoughts I was not aware of a nurse entering the room. She took two vials of blood from me, handed me some papers, told me to read them over, and then sign them. I signed them immediately.

"Let's get this show on the road," I said.

"Yes, sir. We'll need a urine sample. And then the orderly will wheel you down to X-ray and then we'll begin a series of other tests after that."

An orderly arrived, and wheeled me down a long hallway and then into an elevator.

Over an hour later, I was brought up from x-ray and the labs. There was a commotion outside of Running-water's room. Jedediah was standing there with my shotgun, holding off the nursing staff and two security guards. When he saw me, he lowered the gun.

"What's with the gun?" I said.

'They wanted to take Running-water out and cut on him again. I told them no. Adam, you have to give Marrie some time. She's conjuring."

"Conjuring?"

"Yes. She has a way about her much like you do."

Strange, she never did any such thing while I was with her, I thought.

"There really isn't much time. He needs a new kidney and they are seeing if one of mine will work."

"You have healed me as well as others. Why have you given up on my grandson, your friend? Do you have so little faith?" Jedediah said.

"Step aside, Jedediah," I said, pushing the door open.

The room smelled of sage and sweet grass. Running-water's bed now faced the window.

The most awful smell assaulted my nose as I approached his bed. He was lathered in a rancid oil from head to toe. The medical staff had followed us into the room and was really pissed at what they saw, candles were burning, a small smudge pot was smoking.

A nurse started to put up a real fuss.

"What in the world do you think you are doing?" She said.

A glare from Marrie silenced her.

Pointing out the window, Jedediah said, "Look, Adam."

I looked out the window into a parking lot. It was dark. Not even one pole light was on. Then, upon some prearranged signal, the whole area flamed with hundreds of candles, each lit one after the other, outlining a perfect circle of shadowy figures joined together.

I opened the window and the slow deliberate beat of an Indian medicine drum floated up to us.

"My god, there must be a couple hundred people out there. By the sounds of the drums, they must be Natives."

I leaned into the open window. The drum stopped and then began again. As it did, the human chain began to move in sync with the drum beat. It was then that I realized there was an inner circle moving counter to the outer circle. As the drummer increased his tempo, the people's movements became a trot, changing directions without changing their rhythm.

At first, the chanting was barely audible, a whispered 'hu-hu-hu-hu' and like the speed of the dancers, it increased in pitch. I could feel the cadence massaging my heart, my own breathing quickened, and my whole body vibrated in a harmonious interplay with all life forms. Deep within my soul, I heard the eagle's call, I answered it, and at the same time, my body shuddered in protest and I didn't understand why.

"Good lord, look at him! He's almost transparent. Radiating blue light," a nurse said.

An aurora bathed the room. Everything began surreal.

I placed my hands over Running-water's body, not touching his oiled skin. Slowly I moved them from his head to his feet, pausing from time to time, letting the heat from my hands jump to him. Each time my hands came to one of his kidneys, they grew hotter. Unlike before, they did not have the orange-red glow but were now an intense blue-white. My fingers vibrated in time with the drumming. Vibrant colors flashed and bounced around Running-water's body.

The drum and chanting stopped.

My hands cooled and returned to their normal state.

No one in the room made a sound. All was silent.

For just an instant, I thought heard purring. Then I saw its shadow. It darted across the wall behind Running-water's bed.

That's impossible, I thought. It just couldn't be. I left that cougar in Nevada. "Adam."

It was Jedediah calling me. He motioned me to the window. The lights were on and I could see hundreds of people standing, looking up at our window. I placed my hand, palm, outward, on the glass. They raised theirs in return.

"What's the show out there, brother?" Running-water said.

"Come and see for yourself," I said as I helped him off the bed and eased him over to the window.

We stood there; our arms around each other. Grateful. Knowing that life had passed between us and knowing it had been returned. We both waved and a roar went up from the crowd. As we turned back to the room, Running-water grabbed me around the neck and hugged me. A tear formed and fell down his still very pale face.

"Thank you, Adam."

Jedediah began hugging grabbed us both and gave us a bear hug. I glanced around and noticed Marrie standing aloof, staring off into space.

"Unto to thee, oh, Lord." Jedediah said, "Unto to thee."

We helped Running-water back into bed. Marrie seemed to come back from wherever she was and ordered the nurses to turn the bed back to where it had been. She then told them to bring a pot of boiling water, a cup, and a spoon.

In all the excitement, I had not noticed that Marrie was walking. She didn't even have a cane.

"Marrie, you're walking. When? How?" I said.

Evidently, she didn't hear my questions because she was busy at Running-water's bed.

A nurse's aide returned with the hot water, cup, and spoon Marrie had requested. She immediately began to make an herbal tea ignoring the Chief of Staff, Dr. Ann Milford who had come in with the nurse's aide. I introduced her to Marrie and Jedediah. Marrie grunted. Dr. Milford thanked them for their help and then proceeded to check Running-water. Some color had returned to his cheeks and his heart rate had begun to normalize, however, Running-water still showed some signs of jaundice and sallowness about his eyes. The surgeon came in, spoke to Dr. Milford and then the two of them held a whispered conference. Once they had finished their discussion, the surgeon also checked Running-water.

"I'd like to run some tests in a day or two. In the meantime, I think a slow drip of antibiotics is in order. That was some show out front. Who were those people and where did they come from?"

"First people. From the world. And it wasn't a show, young man," Jedediah said.

"I meant no offense. I was fascinated by the display, nothing more," The surgeon said. "What is that peculiar smell? "

A tea to help strengthen the immune system," Marrie said.

"I see," the surgeon said shaking his head as he left the room.

"Adam, may I speak to you for a moment, privately?" Dr. Milford said.

As we stepped out into the hallway she whispered, "Your friend has the smell of death all about him. Did you not smell it?"

"Not death, doc," I said, laughing. "According to Marrie, it's just good old fashion skunk oil. She gave Running-water a rub down with it. It has equally strong healing powers. At least, so Marrie says."

"I don't know about that, but I do strongly suggest a good hot shower; get him some fresh bed clothes. I'll have the orderly come in and change the bedding. That stuff is enough to kill a horse."

"Thanks, doc. I'm sure he will welcome that."

I decided to stay at the hospital and offered Jedediah and Marrie the use of the motor home so they too could stay close by. Jedediah was genuinely pleased with the prospect. He and Marrie left the hospital.

Shortly after Running-water had showered down, gotten on clean clothes and back in bed, I went out to the motor home.

Marrie and Jedediah found the luxurious interior very impressive. We ate a light meal. Marrie said nothing during our meal. I was going to ask her about her walking but she was agitated for some reason.

"I'm going to bed," Marrie announced, getting up from the table.

Jedediah, however, was in no hurry to retire. He was in a talkative mood.

"Tell me about this healing power you have. When did you know you could do such things?"

"Actually, I don't know when I became a healer. The first experience at healing was with the cab driver when I attended the funeral of a friend. Marrie was the second. There had been other times when I seemed to have an impact on people who were ill. I just didn't equate it with being a healer. But long before then I was aware that I intuitively knew things," I said.

"What kind of things?" Jedediah said.

"Probably the first recollection would take me back to a trip into Canada with my parents. We were on a dirt road; my father called it a cow path. I was in the front seat and my father was driving. I told him that a car was going to come around the next curve and smash into us. I laid down on the seat. Within a minute, a car hit us head on. Did a lot of damage to the front end. There are a number of such incidents throughout my life. A more recent example involved the ranger at Tahoe. I knew he had taken the money from Esaugetuh's wallet and I knew that he would tell me he had taken it. While Running-water and I were driving back from the airport at Flagstaff, I kept seeing flames, exploding. There, I used the remote to start the car and it exploded."

"In there," Jedediah said pointing at the hospital, "you seemed to become translucent, turning into a blue-white light. Has that happened to you before?"

"Yes. The first time I wasn't aware of it myself but was told about it later. I was at Lake Tahoe, sitting in the woods, stark naked when the ranger and a sheriff found me sitting in a circle of stones. They said I had a blue light about me; they said I was almost transparent. I had a vague sense of the light while I was in the resonating chamber at Saint-Michaels'. However, I was not aware of the light in the hospital. I've been aware of color changes in my hands while doing a healing."

"Have you ever heard of Adam Kadmon?" Jedediah said.

"No. Who is he?" I said.

"If I recall correctly, in Jewish literature, Adam Kadmon means Divine Light. The two words allude to the nature of being: created being and in this case, Adam, and a primordial manifestation of Divinity, that is, both spirit and flesh personified."

"What's that got to do with me?"

"Some believe that Adam Kadmon is an integrated light body that allows human beings to enter another dimension and to change reality, a merkabah. You seem to become light and you seem to be able to foretell future events, even change them. There is no question that you change present situations. Esaugetuh said you were very powerful."

"Hold on one damn minute! I'm no Divinity. It's true that I seem to be able to do certain kinds of things that others do not do. I don't know the source of my abilities nor what they may or may not involve. I do know that I'm not a parlor trickster who performs for a set fee."

"No need to get in a huff. I'm asking these questions to help you. If I recall correctly, asking questions was one of your particular identifying characteristics."

"Your right," I said sheepishly. "We learn by asking questions. Fire away."

"Have you ever felt you have traveled in what is called parallel universes?" Jedediah said.

"I've had what you might call an other world experience. I had not thought of it as being in a parallel universe, in another dimension."

"It's my understanding, and it is limited, that there are parallel worlds and that in these, exist all experience, and the mind, the human mind, and is in each of these worlds," Jedediah said.

"Esaugetuh used to talk of such things. He used to say that all possibilities existed at the same time. Socrates said all you had to do was to ask the right question. Esaugetuh, however, always said that I had to change my perspective and perception in order to get at the right question and then the answer."

"Can you change your perspective enough to move into another existing parallel universe?"

"I don't know. I don't even know how to begin such a thing."

"Want to try a little experiment?" Jedediah said.

"The last time someone said that nearly got me killed."

"Well, this is a more of an inquiry rather than a scientific experiment."

"Okay. What have you got in mind?"

"Let's begin by using memory recall. I want you to go back in your memories and locate those experiences from which you have learned something of value to you."

"Ah, a little Adlerian psychology. How far back do you want me to go?"

"Begin with the time you spent with Esaugetuh until a couple of hours ago in Running-water's room. Speaking of, don't you think we ought to check on him?"

"He's resting and healing nicely."

"How do you know that? You haven't left here or phoned the hospital."

"I just know. I communicate with him just as Esaugetuh does with me sometimes only with Running-water there are no words."

"What did you see in the hospital before my Marrie and I arrived?"

"I saw Running-water's soul and I cried. Something I didn't even do for my parents."

"That tells me a great deal. You are a spirit walker. Besides crying when you saw my grandson's soul what else did you do?" Marrie said as she came from the bedroom.

"I cried out."

"Did you touch his soul?" Marrie said.

"Is that something of importance, Marrie?" Jedediah said.

"Yes, very important. Try to remember, Adam. Did you touch his soul?"

"Yes, I grabbed it and held on as it tried to leave. At one point I think I wrapped it in my arms and forced it back to Running-water."

"Oh, my! Oh, my!" Marrie said.

"What?" I said.

"Yes, Marrie, what, for heaven's sake?" Jedediah said.

"In the old days, long before the white man, there were certain members of my people who had great powers. Some were generally feared because they were soul snatchers. However, one among them returned the soul to a chosen one. Once this soul was returned that person was destined to have a very long life, to live many, many years, alone and childless. The people often referred to this person as an IT because it never sought a mate. You have sealed the end of my line."

"What the hell would you have me do? Would you have had me let him die?" "We still have our granddaughter, Running-water's twin. Does she not carry our blood line, Marrie?"

"The line is carried by the male," Marrie said.

"That's a lot of crap," I said.

"I'm afraid my dear Marrie, I must agree with Adam. Biology tells us differently," Jedediah said.

"Marrie is Esaugetuh an IT? That's why he adopted me, isn't it?"

"I don't know. It's possible. I have no proof that he ever married or that he had children. I know of no woman who slept in his tepee. And I don't care what your science says, Mr. College Professor. I know what the Old Ones have said."

"Which is more important, Running-water being alive or not having great grandchildren?" Jedediah said.

"While you two debate that one I'm going back into the hospital and stay with Running-water for a while."

By ten o'clock, the visiting hours were long over; the hospital staff knew I would be coming and going throughout the night. I certainly didn't expect the wild outrage that greeted me when I entered the lobby.

"Good god, do you realize what you have done? You've ruined this hospital."

"And you are?" I asked.

"Night supervisor Jennifer Brown. Get these people the hell out of here and do it now. And don't try to palaver all over me. It won't get you anywhere."

Apparently, word had gotten out about the Native Americans' medicine dance and a large crowd of people had camped in the halls, nooks, and crannies of the hospital. Most were waiting to meet the shaman who brought people back to life.

I was surprised the hospital didn't come and get me the moment this began to happen. That remained a mystery. It was obvious that I couldn't just walk down the hall and into Running-water's room. For a moment, I considered trying a mass hypnosis. I'd not done such a thing but understood it was possible. Because I wasn't sure of the consequences, I changed my mind and I borrowed a white coat, a clipboard, and a stethoscope. Only with considerable difficulty was I able to get into Running-water's room. He was sleeping.

He sensed my presence and started to get up. I signed him not to speak. Quickly I told him of the situation and that I had to do something to resolve the issue. Together we hatched a scheme to get us both out of the mess. I pushed the emergency button and a medical team rushed into the room. We explained what the game plan was.

"Put Running-water on a gurney. Cover him up with a sheet. Let it be understood that he has died. Then have an orderly clean the room, but make sure the door left open so that people in the hallway can see in. Have the orderly make a big deal out of placing Running-water's clothes in a plastic bag." I said to the medical team that had come to the room.

The charade went off without a hitch. We got Running-water out to the motor home without being seen. Drove it down the street a few blocks and stopped.

We would wait there for a while in order to give the hospital time to clear out the crowd. Marrie was insisting that Running-water take the bedroom. She sure could be stubborn and I noted a strange look in her eyes. It was only after I reminded her that she was my guest that she reluctantly gave in.

Soon after she and Jedediah had retired, I called the hospital. The people had cleared out and things had returned to normal state. I wanted the name of a kidney specialist and a referral for Running-water. An appointment was set up through an answering service.

Running-water came up front and sat in the seat next to me.

"How can I ever thank you? What can I ever say to you?" Running-water said.

"You already have," I said.

"How is that?"

"You are here, now, alive! That's good enough for me." I said as I slipped the motor home into gear and headed west.

"Where we heading?" Running-water said.

"Back to the cabin. We'll stay there until I know you are okay."

"You're a regular old mother hen. You're getting as bossy as the 'old one'."

"You mean your grandmother?"

We both chuckled.

I have to admit it struck me as odd that she was more concerned about being a great grandmother than about Running-water's condition. Even though I am not of her culture, I still think a woman's concern would be for the health of her grandchild rather than his ability to procreate. There was still something about her feet and the whole business of conjuring. I just wish I could get all the pieces to fit.

I was so lost in my thoughts I nearly missed the turn into Jedediah's cabin. It took some very careful maneuvering to get the motor home through the bumpy and narrow road. I drove into the open meadow and headed up the road to the cabin. I swear the headlights caught a cougar jumping down from the roof of the cabin. I shook my head in an effort to clear my vision.

Jedediah and Marrie were both in deep sleep. I was surprised the bumpy road hadn't wakened them. Running-water and I each took a bunk. As soon as I heard his breathing steady, I got up, went out to the meadow behind the cabin, and laid down, facing the northern sky.

Memories of past night skies flowed seamlessly before my mind's eye. Memories of late night conversations with Esaugetuh wrapped me in a melancholy reverie. I wish I knew why he wanted me to track down the seven people on the list I found in his wallet he had put at Tahoe. Are they merely a whim on his part? What are their roles? What part do they play? What have I learned through all of this? Questions and more questions. They spin around in my head faster than the numbers in a bingo cage.

A cough off in the distance brought me back. I sensed its presence. My mind told me to get up and run like hell but my instincts told me to remain still. I eased myself into a sitting position, cross-legged, and forcing my body to relax I began to hum "hu-hu-hu-hu," the rhythmic chant sung by the People at the hospital. Keeping the pitch and tone the same I waited. Nothing. I was sure I was having a lucid dream. But then I heard it! The soft low purring. It was sitting right in front of me. Slowly I extended my right hand. It licked my fingers, turned, and disappeared into the waning night. Just for a moment, I thought it had azure blue eyes and like days gone by, I felt their scan.

I laid back down and closed my eyes as the smell of sweet clover and honeysuckle filled the air around me, covering me in a blanket of warmth. Sleep, wonderful, peaceful sleep finally was mine. Either the heat of the noon-day sun or the voice of Jedediah woke me whichever, I was acutely aware of both.

"Wondered where you had got yourself off to. You feel like some breakfast or do you want lunch?"

"How's Running-water?"

"You'll have to ask him yourself. He's not talking much this morning. Acts out of sorts. You two have an argument. That's why you are out here?"

"No. You have any coffee made?" I said.

We went back to the cabin. Running-water was sitting on the step, staring off into space, unaware of our presence. I indicated that I wanted to speak to Running-water alone. Jedediah went into the cabin. I sat down beside Running-water and put my hand on his shoulder.

"Don't touch me. You've touched me enough already. You should have let me die."

"That's the second time it has been suggested that I should have let you die. It had better be the last. To set the record straight you saved your own ass. You willed yourself to live. I had already done all I could do and had prepared myself for your death. No, suppose you cut to the chase and tell me what's this is all about."

"Marrie said you had held my soul in your arms. That I'm condemned. There is no wife or family for me. I'm to live alone, sexless, an IT for the rest of my life."

"Look at me," I said

"No! I'm not ever going to look at you. I'm done with you."

"I don't know about this other stuff Marrie has been feeding you but you are going to listen to what I have to say. You understand?"

"Have your say and get it over with."

Yes, I held your soul in my arms with all the brotherly love I could muster. I called upon everything divine in the world, in the universe itself. It didn't seem to be enough. You continued to slip away. So then, I offered the only thing left, myself. Your soul returned to your body and your life forces once again began to flow."

"Marrie says that's a lot of bull crap."

"Go ahead, have it your way."

With that said, I went to the motor home, started it up, turned the vehicle around, and headed out. Unlike Orpheus, [13] I didn't look back. Where I'm going I don't know. All I know is that I am on the road again, alone!

CHAPTER 11 - CHRISTINE LILITH CONDUIT

There are "innumerable worlds in the Boundless."
Anaximander

I didn't expect them to come after me and they didn't. Once out on the main road, I headed north. A phone call to Dutch and Brett let them know I was moving on. It was then that I realized that Running-water's gear was still on board. I stopped in town, went to Sheriff Logan's office, and asked him if I could leave it there.

I took the remainder of the cash along with the signed deed to the cabin and the property, tucked both in his backpack. I asked Sheriff Logan if he would let Jedediah know. I didn't want Running-water to think I was keeping his stuff as a means of getting him to come after me. Before leaving town, I filled up with gas, fresh water, and picked up several maps.

Even though there were still two names left on my list, I wasn't in any hurry to begin the search for them. I wanted time alone; time to think, and to let all that has happened to coalesce. It wouldn't have done any good to tell Running-water that he was not the one destined to be alone.

I am!

He wouldn't have accepted that from me in his present mood. In my mind, Vermont seemed to offer just the right mixture of the natural world, quaint towns, and opportunities for private time.

I remembered a Vermont travelogue showing a beautiful lake snuggled between two mountains. The narrator said it was a place once visited by Rudyard

Kipling, Robert Frost, and other famous people in the world of literature. Perhaps, like them, I too can find the magic of the muses. It's like James Joyce said, 'I go to encounter for the millionth time the reality of experience.' After all, there is more to the sky than meets the mountain.

Rather than heading east and then through Connecticut, New Hampshire, or Massachusetts, I headed into New York State. I left the Thruway at Albany and headed into Bennington. From there I headed north to Rutland. I spent the night near there at an RV park. With the sunrise, I was on my way to White River Junction to pick up US 91 and on to St. Johnsbury. From St. Johnsbury I headed north to Lake Willoughby. Some people call it the Lake Lucerne of North America. Longer than it is wide, Willoughby is nestled between Mount Pisgah and Mount Hoar. Its banks appear to be dotted with private camps however at the north end of the lake I found an open area with picnic tables. I backed the motor home in, shut it down, got out, and gave my legs a much needed stretching.

In the Northeast Kingdom of Vermont, there are many excellent hiking trails and they will be most welcome as I try to sort out all that has transpired in my life. I was walking along the shoreline when I heard the siren. A State Patrol had stopped at the road's edge. The officer motioned for me to come up to the road. As I approached his vehicle, he got out of the car. He was a tall man in his mid-thirties.

"That your motor home?"

"Yes. Is there something wrong?" I said.

"You can't park there overnight. It's strictly a picnic area."

"Are there any campsites around the lake?"

"Not around the lake, but down the road a ways you'll find a camp ground. If you like, I'll call and see if they have a slot to accommodate your rig. That sure is a fancy outfit."

"Thanks. I'd appreciate that."

"Going to be here long?"

"I don't know. Maybe a couple of weeks. I want to do some hiking."

The patrolman called the camp ground. They could handle my large motor home. He gave me specific directions and then left. A few miles later I was pulling into the site, had a slot assigned to me, a copy of the rules and regulations, and a hearty welcome. After a quick meal and a hot shower, I hit the sack; Tomorrow, hiking.

Morning brought me a new interest. As I was going through the duffle bag that had contained the money, I found the notebook I had picked up from the bags of stuff brought from the trawler St. Michaels had sunk. It not only contained dates with cash amounts beside them but also names. One really focused my attention. It was the same as one of the two remaining names on my list and with it was a telephone number. As hard as I tried, I could not force myself to ignore this coincidence. I called Christine Lilith Conduit. I got a recording for a bookstore. I left a brief message with my number.

I put a bottle of water, a light snack, a map of hiking trails, an extra pair of socks, and my first aid kit into my back pack, then locked the motor home and headed back toward Willoughby Lake.

It was bugging me that Christine Lilith Conduit's name and telephone number should be in a notebook belonging to a now deceased scum bag of a sea captain. The captain and his crew were originally hired by Randolph to blow me up. Then, he and some of his crew in cahoots with Kim Su tried to wipe out Saint-Michaels, his staff, Running-water and myself. There was no notation of money after her name. What was her connection to Esaugetuh and does that imply that there was a connection between the captain and Esaugetuh as well?

So wrapped up in my speculations it didn't register with me that I should have been enjoying the beautiful Vermont countryside. I was on Mount Pisgah looking down on Lake Willoughby. It was a blue ribbon, glacier-cut through the mountains, surrounded by lush green forest; a mirror reflecting the sky above and simultaneously suggesting mystery beneath its glassy surface. If indeed there were muses, surely they would be here, in this place, in this time. It was a short lived reverie.

A gaggle of laughing Girl Scouts burst upon the scene. Seeing me, they froze and became quiet. I guess their leaders didn't expect to find anyone because my presence seemed to make them nervous. I nodded and began my trek back to camp. The sun was well into its decline by the time I reached the camp ground.

I called the number for Christine Lilith Conduit again. Instead of a recording, I got a live voice. She was at a college in Vermont giving a series of lectures on channeling, teleportation, and the transmigration of souls.

That might be her connection to Esaugetuh, I thought, but I wonder what the connection is to the dead ship's captain.

Dr. Conduit was staying in Montpelier, about three hours from the lake. She graciously agreed to set aside some time for me to meet with her if I would meet there.

After my evening meal, I headed to Montpelier. I wanted to be sure that I would be there early in the morning to meet her for breakfast. I explained I would be driving a forty foot red and black motor home.

The trip to Montpelier was an easy ride. I found an RV park just outside of the city, rented a slot and bedded down for the night. The next morning I was on my way into the city, looking for a mall that allowed motor homes to park. I telephoned Christine to tell her where I was located. She laughed.

"What's so funny?"

"I'm in the laundry right in front of you. I can see you. Talk about coincidence."

"Breakfast will soon be ready, come on over," I said.

I watched her walking toward the coach. She was a tall slender woman with carrot red hair. I opened the door, and the steps dropped so she could enter.

"I've wanted to get a good look at one of these. Thought it would be nice to have one to live in while I am doing a lecture tour. What's the price on one like this?

"Five hundred thousand."

"Way out of my league. How may I help you?" Christine said.

"As I explained on the phone, I found your name in a record book belonging to a captain of a trawler that was sunk out in the Atlantic Ocean. Of all the names, yours was the only one that did not have a dollar amount assigned to it. Second, I found your name on a slip of paper belonging to a friend of mine. A person in the FBI located your address for me.

"Well, I don't know of any sea captain but that doesn't mean anything because of the number of clients I have had over the years. I would be happy to check those once I am back home. Is there a particular reason you are interested in this information?"

"Yes, the captain attempted to murder me. Esaugetuh, my friend, and mentor is missing. I've been trying to find him. I feel there's a connection."

"Esaugetuh! Oh, my god! He's missing. How horrible! When?"

"You know him, then?"

"Yes. What a wonderful man. We met several years ago in Peru. He was giving a presentation on Ancient Spirituality and I was giving a talk on Interconnectedness at the same symposium. We became good friends and stayed in touch with each other," Christine said.

"When was the last time you heard from him?" I said, turning the French toast I was cooking.

"Hmm, that smells wonderful. It's been three or four years. Actually, closer to five. He said he would be gone for quite a while because he was taking a trip. Oh, my god. You're his son— Adam. I just didn't make the connection. I am so sorry, the sea captain business threw me off.

"He was my mentor and teacher. He adopted me at an Indian ceremony at Mesa Verde. I am very worried that something has happened to him."

"I understand you have—."

"Breakfast is ready," I said. placing a stack of French toast on the table. "Hot cinnamon syrup coming right up."

She agreed to meet with me that evening and we would do a combined channeling. She had a lecture to give at ten that morning and again at two in the afternoon. I gave her the directions to the RV site.

"Perhaps if both of us use our talents we can connect with Esaugetuh. It's worth a try, I said as she left.

That leaves one person on the list. If that person provides no clues as to the whereabouts of Esaugetuh, I'm not sure what to do. I'm still don't have a handle on why he had the list. Maybe, he didn't want me to do anything with the list. Maybe it was just for his own information. That's a real possibility, I thought.

My ringing phone interrupted and slipped on my thoughts. It was Dutch. He said an insurance agent had called and wanted to know where to send the check. I told him to have the agent contact Running-water. As far as I was concerned, he was still my attorney.

"Listen, I want you to bring the jet to Burlington, Vermont. Stand by to fly me out of there. The notice may be short."

"No problem. I'll give you a call when we arrive," Dutch said.

After that, I began preparing myself for the evening with Christine. The cell phone and the radio phone of the motor home were turned off. I wanted no interruptions as she attempted to channel and to make a connection with my inner being.

I burned some sage and smudged it over my body. Next, I lit a braid of sweet grass and fanned it throughout the motor home. I bathed and then rubbed down with lemon oil mixed with angelica root. I sat down, cross-legged, and began to pray.

I prayed to the Spirits of the Four Corners of the earth, asking them for guidance. I offered them the traditional pipe and tobacco as a symbol of my respect. I called upon my eagle spirit for support and comfort.

During this time, I ate and drank nothing. Continued meditation further quieted my soul, clearing my mind of clutter, and making me open to spiritual tranquility.

Around ten that evening Christine arrived. My nakedness startled her. I apologized. I felt her gaze linger as I slipped on a robe.

"I don't work with people who are into drugs. I'm sorry I misunderstood your intentions," Christine said.

"There are no drugs here. What you smell is sage. It is used in sacred ceremonies. Then there is sweet grass to help with purification and on my body, there is lemon oil and angelica root to attract good Spirits. I thought you understood Native ways. I had hoped you could help me find my friend, my mentor, my father. I seem to be the one who has misunderstood."

"We do seem to have gotten off on the wrong foot. I wasn't expecting you to be naked and it threw me."

"I'll try if you still want me to. Sorry I misjudged you."

"We need to get rid of the tension; clear the air, so to speak. That may take time. I've fasted all afternoon as well as prayed. Perhaps we can meditate together and establish a new bond."

With that said, I patted the pillow beside me, indicating that she should sit. Both of us sat quietly regulating our breathing and clearing our minds. The joining, if we were successful, would be immediate. If it didn't occur immediately, there would be no use in continuing.

She held out her hands, palms up. I laid mine on top of hers. Our eyes met, locked. A simultaneous flash filled the room.

For one marvelous nanosecond, I was aware of being propelled at an unimaginable speed. Then I had a feeling of a loud clap of thunder vibrating against my chest, yet hearing nothing. At that precise moment, I realized I had been sundered into another dimension–one described by Plato in his *Republic*–where the beginnings of all beginnings began, the world of Ananke. I was standing on the edge of a giant whorl [14], hollow in its nature and looking down I could count seven lesser whirlpools moving at slower speeds. The seventh I recognized as our sun. The same circular motion was evident for the giant vortex and yet the seven inner whirlpools moved in the opposite direction and at a slower speed. The motion of the vortex caught my foot and I was plunged into its center. There, I found myself in a world exactly like the one I had been in, yet so unalike at the same time. Time? There is no time. All things are by Necessity!

It soon became apparent that I could move around but in a lightened state similar to that which the astronauts feel as weightlessness. I learned my center and stayed grounded. Voices from every direction painfully assaulted my ears; some were garbled, some low, and some high pitched.

All sounds intensified. Gradually, I was able to sort them out, to tune into individual sounds and then voices. Then I heard my own voice crying out, "Esaugetuh where are you?"

No answer. I felt pretty stupid standing in the middle of the road shouting at the top of my lungs. I started to move on across the street when I heard a car horn, but it was too late to get out of the way. I froze. Panic gripped me as the car with its breaks squealing rolled right through me.

I caught a glimpse of the people in the car as it flashed by; their mouths agape, they looked like they had seen a ghost. Once the car stopped, the driver of the car jumped out, screaming at me.

"You stupid son-of-a-bitch. You on loco weed?"

"You could have killed me. Then you would have been in serious trouble.

Good thing I was able to jump out of the way," I said.

"Yeah, well, next time watch where you're walking."

What an odd sensation. I felt I had a solid body, yet obviously, I didn't and yet, I still felt very visible. I wonder what H. G. Wells would have done with this kind of information. I still fondly remember reading his *The Invisible Man* when I was in junior high school.

Hmm, wonder if I can walk through walls. No. Stay focused. Esaugetuh must remain my focal point. I want to find him or at least communicate with him. The questions, always the questions: How should I begin? Where should I begin?

"Begin at the beginning," Christine said.

"Where are you?" I said.

"In your mind."

"Okay, so I how I get back to Lake Tahoe?"

"Broaden your search. Lake Tahoe may be too narrow. Use your mind to project yourself. Remember you transfer energy to heal, use it to propel yourself," Christine said.

It's all so strange. I don't know where I am or what year or day it is. I do know that if I want to find Esaugetuh I have to concentrate with my total being. It doesn't matter where I am.

A small park nearby seemed to be to be an ideal quiet place to sit and concentrate. A church, Spanish in style, was directly across the street. I considered that but either a wedding or a baptism was going on because of the number of people going in who were all dressed up and in a festive mood.

A gazebo in the middle of the park seemed to offer the best place for quiet solitude. It was large, the kind bands use to present Sunday afternoon concerts and politicians use as a speaker's platform as they stump for votes.

Four wide brick steps with wrought iron handrails lead to its interior. Crushed stone, orange in color, made a walkway around the gazebo. Trees, sparse as they were, dotted the park and seemed to emphasize its starkness. No one seemed to be at the gazebo so I went over, sat down on one of the steps, and tried to quiet my mind.

That didn't happen. I saw a flash with my left eye and another with my right, instantly. Perhaps, sensing a flash better describes what was going on. The left eye sensed a red stream and the right eye a blue one and then everything in front of me turned to dull gray— colorless actually —just as the world would be if one were dead. However, people, as well as leaves on trees, were moving. The whole panorama faded in and out, folding and opening like a handheld Japanese fan.

All of which made it very difficult for me to concentrate. Old memories of advice from Esaugetuh came flooding back: *Act out of Necessity, don't force, but accept, and gently provide direction.*

Out of Necessity. Plato and Ananke again. According to the old story, the Spindle of Life turns on the knees of Necessity and that on the upper level of each vortex sits a siren who circles with her vortex, humming one sound. All of the sirens humming together produce a unified harmony.

It is that unified harmony that I must achieve in my body, spirit, and soul. I stretched my legs out in front of me, leaned back, and looked up at a tangerine colored sky. Totally bizarre! The leaves on the trees were now purple; their trunks a golden color that would have made Cortez and his men truly believe they had found the city of gold.

Instantly, they were all death-gray, hauntingly sallow. Obviously, there was some kind of a fluctuation going on and I'm not sure if it's my energy level or that of Christine's or something out of our control.

Whatever I am going to do and I better do it quickly. I closed my eyes, took a deep breath, and tried to mind walk the world I was now in. Moving from north to south, then to east and west, I called his name.

Nothing! I tried again. Then I heard it! His voice!

"Why do you call me? More questions?"

"I–."

"You have the answers. Open your mind to receive them."

"I wanted to tell you that I–."

"I know. I love you, too, son. There's something else I've meant to tell you."

"What? Tell me what it is you want of me. For god's sake. No, for my sake, tell me!"

"You don't understand. You don't need me. You can now walk not only among the living but also among those who are waiting to be born as well as those who have gone on. Remember this, there can be only one."

"Adam," Christine called. "Adam, can you hear me?"

I opened my eyes and she was still holding my hands. A look of total consternation filled her gaunt face.

"You're dripping wet. Are you okay?"

"Whew! That was some experience. Are you as drained as I am?"

"Did you find Esaugetuh?" Christine said.

"Yes. But I'm not sure where he is. I think he's somewhere west."

"And he is alive?"

"I'm not sure."

"What do you mean you're not sure?"

"I don't know if he's dead or alive. How do you tell the difference?"

"Did his voice sound hollow or did it sound vibrant?" Christine said.

"I can't really say. His voice was distant; his comments were short and almost hostile."

"Hmm. Generally, a vibrancy in one's voice means the individual is alive." Christine said.

"If blunt can be construed as vibrant I guess he's alive somewhere, but I still don't know where."

"Perhaps the next person on your list will be able to help you. I don't think I can do anything more for you.

I'm really quite tired and it's been a long day. If you don't mind I'll leave now."

"Of course. Thank you, Christine. I really appreciate your help. By the way, you do not have stomach cancer." I said.

"How?"

"I did a scan, and Christine, I also know that you have considered suicide. It is never an option. Get some help. Ulcers can be cured," I said as she left.

I called Dutch to have him bring the jet to Burlington where I would meet him. From there we would head west to Reno. I had some unfinished business there.

CHAPTER 12 - UNFINISHED BUSINESS

Like harmony in music; there is a dark inscrutable workmanship that reconciles Discordant elements, makes them cling together.
William Wordsworth

I took my time going to Burlington. Because of the size of the motor home, a slower speed over the Vermont roads was required. I was glad because the scenery along the way was so beautiful I wanted to enjoy it. Each part of our country has places of natural beauty and Vermont has been no exception. By the time I got to Burlington, I had changed my mind as to where I wanted to go. Instead of going to Reno, I decided that a visit to Albuquerque might prove to be more fruitful.

I don't know if Running-water would be there or not, but it would give me the opportunity to check up on him, to locate his law office, and to check out the newspaper for which he wrote. It was a screwy idea but I felt something positive would come of it.

It was good to see Dutch and Brett once again. They had had no communication from Running-water, Jedediah, or Marrie.

"You want to place a call to Running-water?" Dutch said.

I declined, pretending not to see his quizzical look. Running-water's words still hurt. Perhaps it was his tone more than the words. Maybe both. The cut was deeper than I wanted to admit.

I really missed him but I wasn't willing to admit that I had the power to make it different. If I forced him to come back, that would be an abuse of my powers and that would violate the sanctity of my vision quest.

What harm would a phone call do, I thought. No, damn it! He was the one who shot off his mouth, not me. Let him call me.

I felt a sudden pain in my side. It was sharp enough to make me grimace. I haven't felt that for a while.

Albuquerque would be a nice change. It's a beautiful southwestern city of nearly a half million people. Native American and Mexican influences provide a natural harmony that permeates the culture.

Dutch brought the jet down at Albuquerque International Sunport, which was about four miles southeast of the city's central business district. A rental car was waiting for us. We made an exit off of Sunport Boulevard to I-25 and headed northeast to the city. I made reservations at a downtown hotel for the three of us, each with a room of his own.

Old habits die hard. I hadn't realized how much I had grown to depend on Running-water as my protector and back-up. I had thought a nap after a hot shower would energize me after our flight. As much as I wanted it, sleep would not come.

The phone rang ending any further effort at resting. Dutch wanted to know if I had something for them to do and if not, would I join them in doing the city. I didn't have anything for them to do and declined their invitation. I called the front desk and ordered a rental delivered to the hotel.

I got up and began to thumb the yellow pages. No Paul Dakota, attorney, was listed. Next, I checked the listing for attorneys and didn't find his name there. Nor did I find his name in the white pages. I then looked up Running-water and various combinations of his Christian and Indian names. Nothing. Since it was just midday, I called the New Mexico Bar Association. They had no such person. They did inform me that not all attorneys in New Mexico were members. They further suggested that I check some of the charitable organizations. Frequently young attorneys will work for the charities to gain experience and to build their vitae.

At the hotel lobby, a conversation with the Concierge got me a listing of local charities and their telephone numbers. Additionally, I was able to get the name of a local Native American Newspaper. A charity for the homeless struck my fancy and I called its number. A Paul Dakota had done free legal work for them. He had not been in for quite some time. They suggested I contact the alum association of the University's law school. I got an address north of the city.

Before leaving, I called the newspaper. They didn't know where he was. Hadn't had anything from him in over a year. Their address matched the one from the Alumni Association.

Before starting out on my search for Runningwater's history, I decided to take a long walk to think things through. Talk about déjà vu!

Within a few blocks of my hotel, I saw the park with the gazebo from my parallel universe experience. Here its name is Old Town Plaza. Even the Spanish-style church was there. The trees were normal, not the gold and purple I had seen earlier. I went over to the gazebo, counted five steps and they had the wrought iron hand railing. I sat down just to get the feel of the place once again, only this time, in a normal experiential way. The midday sun warmed me. Somewhere, I thought, here in Albuquerque I will find Esaugetuh. Maybe at Runningwater's apartment?

The rental had a Global Positioning System and finding the address was relatively easy. The apartment building was a two story southwestern adobe style architecture. A fountain and cacti accented a semicircular drive in front of the building. Just to the right was a swimming pool and on the left was a series of covered stalls for the tenants' cars. I noted that there wasn't a car in the stall assigned to his apartment. I found the manager, greased his palm with a couple bills. He let me into Running-water's apartment.

Modestly furnished in contemporary southwestern furniture and accents, it was a typical bachelor's pad. It was neat, almost too neat. For an apartment unoccupied, for months, there would have been some dust on the furniture but there was none. A check of the bedroom revealed further neatness, the closet contained a couple of suits, some shirts, and other apparel. Dresser drawers contained socks, underwear, and a couple boxes of condoms, sweaters neatly folded.

I next checked the bathroom. A partially used shower soap bar still hung on its rope over the shower head, and the towels were fresh. A small balcony with sliding glass doors opened from the bedroom. All that was there was one lawn chair and a small table. I almost missed it, a cigarette butt laying on the floor next to the table. Running-water doesn't smoke.

I picked it up, noted lipstick and brand. The kitchen was my next stop. Nothing in the refrigerator. Obviously, no one was living here. The lack of dust on tables still bothered me. Where is his mail? Somebody must be picking it up. Another thing that bothered me was the lack of any really personal items: college degrees not apparent, no college yearbooks, no photos of family or buddies, and no trophies.

I went back to the bedroom and the clothes closet. The few shirts were new as were the suits. One still had a tag on the inside sleeve. They didn't seem to be of the correct size to fit a man of Running-water's size. I heard the door open and ducked back into the closet and waited.

I waited. I heard no voices, no further movement. Slowly I opened the closet, stepped into the bedroom, and inched my way to the bedroom door. Cautiously I peeked around the corner. Sitting in one of the two living room chairs was a man, forty-something, reading a newspaper.

"Move and you're dead," I said.

"It's okay, mister. Stay calm. Don't shoot."

"Who are you and what are you doing here?" I said as I stepped the rest of the way into the living room.

"You want my money? Here take my wallet. There's a grand in it."

"It's not your money I want. I asked who you were."

"Gordon Alexander is my name. Say, don't I know you from somewhere? You a friend of Paul, my nephew?"

"Running-water mentioned he had an uncle, but never said his name."

"You must be Adam. Glad to meet you." Alex said extending his hand.

"I may or may not be. I want to know what you are doing here."

"I keep this place for Paul and me to use when we are in the city. If you need a place there's room here."

"No. I have a hotel. Do you know Esaugetuh?"

"You haven't said who you are and put that damn gun away."

"I am Adam," I said, holstering the gun.

"Running-water told me he was going to try and find you. I recognized you from the videos."

"Videos?"

"Yeah. He has several. So, where's that wayward nephew of mine? I haven't heard from him in months."

"The last I knew he was with his grandparents. How is it I can find no record of his law degree or law firm?"

"Grandparents? His grandparents have been dead for years."

"No. His grandfather is Jedediah Woods and his grandmother is Marrie Copa. Running-water's father was their child born out of wedlock. He was given up, raised by another family, and later killed in Viet Nam. Now then, what about this law business?"

"I'm an attorney. Running-water is an attorney in my office. He's not a partner yet but will be if he ever comes back and gets to work."

"What about his twin sister?"

"Ah! That one! She is absolutely beautiful and totally independent. I doubt if any man will ever tame her. You have an interest?"

"No. I asked you if you knew Esaugetuh. Do you?"

"No. Just heard of him. He's a powerful shaman out of Canada."

"Where is your practice located?"

"Northwest of here, just this side of Gallup. Route 66 territory."

"Does Running-water have a place there?"

"He lives with me. My wife died a few years ago. We have no kids and Running-water has always been special to us. Teachers here don't make a whole lot of money, so my late wife and I helped put him through law school."

"And not Daphne?"

"I said she was one independent young lady. Wouldn't let us."

"I want to call on Running-water's mother, Cornelia. I understand she teaches here in Albuquerque. Do you know where?"

"Not the specific school. Of course, I know where she lives. If you want, we can go over there now. We might catch her before she leaves for her swimming or yoga class," Gordon said.

"Hmm. It might be a good idea if you did go with me. The news that she has a father and mother-in-law living might be a shock."

"So you're saying Paul's father was given away by this couple."

"No, he was given away by Marrie's parents who were paid to leave town by her lover's parents. Jedediah never knew he had a son. It's the kind of story that's made for TV movies."

"I'd sure like to hear the whole story sometime," Gordon said.

"No problem. How about those videos? I'd like to see them.

It was uncanny seeing the shots of Esaugetuh. I don't know who I miss more, Running-water, or Esaugetuh. I never knew that we were being taped. Even our voices had been recorded. I certainly wasn't a very observant person, that's for sure.

About half way through the fifth tape, I spotted the two men that tried to ambush Running-water and me in Arizona. Their voices were clear. It's unbelievable but it appears they were going to attempt to kill me there but changed their mind because of the crowd.

Because they said something about waiting until I was on the road again, I wondered if Running-water's flat tire was an accident. I'm sure he never checked back with the rental agency to see why the tire went flat.

"Did Running-water watch these tapes?" I said.

"Gee, I don't know. I only watched the first two. You in some kind of trouble? Sounds like those two guys intend to knock you off."

"Not anymore. They're dead. And that's another story. Do you think Cornelia is home from her swimming or yoga and would see me?"

"Yeah, she's probably home. I don't know about you but I'm hungry. There's nothing here but we can get something on the way if you like."

After a quick stop at a burger place, we were on our way. I called the hotel and left a message for Dutch and Brett. I shuddered at the memory of the last time I left them. From the burger place, it was but a short drive to Cornelia's. Gordon rang the doorbell.

"Evening, Cornelia. I brought someone who wants to meet you. His name is Adam." Gordon said.

"You! You— You're the one responsible for my Paul being away and never a word from him. Go away," Cornelia said as she swung at Adam.

Grabbing and holding her, Gordon said, "That's no way to behave, Cornelia. Adam has news for you. I strongly suggest you calm down."

"What can he possibly say to me? He's responsible for my son being gone for two years and all that time, not one word. For all, I know he could have murdered him."

"Mrs. Dakota, Running-water is staying with his grandparents in Pennsylvania," I said.

"Liar. My parents are dead as are his father's. Gordon, how could you bring this person to my home? For shame!"

"I'm afraid you are mistaken. Surely, you must have known that your late husband was adopted. His biological parents are very much alive; one of whom knew nothing of his existence until a short time ago," I said.

"May we come in or not, Cornelia?" Gordon said.

She stepped back so we could enter.

Once she realized I was not some terrible ogre she was a charming and warm person. Two hours later, I was still telling her all the details of the past two years and especially of Running-water's brush with death.

It seemed totally out of character for Running-water not to have been in contact with his mother during that time. Even though we felt the cell phones were a problem I was sure he would have sent her an e-mail message at least before we realized the computer had been hacked.

"Do you have a computer, Mrs. Dakota?" I said.

"Yes, but I don't use it. It's something Paul thought I should have. It's just too complicated for me. Why?"

"Running-water was at his computer all the time. I'm sure he must have sent you an e-mail. Where is your machine? We can check it if you like

Sure enough. There were dozens of e-mail messages from Running-water. Cornelia was more than embarrassed.

"Oh my! I am so ashamed. Please forgive me. I don't know what to say."

"Would you like to meet your in-laws and see Running-water?" I said.

"Yes! It would be really nice, but I don't see how I can. I can't afford to go traipsing across the country."

"How soon can you be ready to leave? I'll have my pilot fly you there."

"You own a plane and have a pilot to boot?" Gordon said.

"A Gulfstream Jet. It's at the Albuquerque International Sunport. I can have it ready to take off within a few hours."

Cornelia was ecstatic. She called her school's emergency

number and got a substitute for three days.

"This is so unbelievable. Just like in the Soaps. I am so sorry I was rude to you. Please, please forgive me," Cornelia said.

"No problems. We'll not bring it up again."

Two phone calls got everything in motion: One call t Dutch and the other to Jedediah. Jedediah never mentioned Running-water and I didn't ask. A coolness in his demeanor told me not to pursue any further conversation.

Sometimes when you do for people, it is resented because it makes them feel obligated. Maybe I did that to Jedediah. Maybe I ruined his paradise by adding all the modern fixtures. It was not my intent and I hope he realizes that.

I dropped Gordon back at his apartment and headed back to my hotel. Dutch and Brett had already gone back to the airport. I had asked Gordon for the video tapes and had decided to go through the rest of them. Listening to Esaugetuh's voice again was unsettling. Listening to my own words brought home one very clear message: I sure was one dumb ass!

"Was?" I thought to myself. "Man, you still are."

"Yes. You are one dumb ass!"

"Who's there?" I said.

"You know the story of Humpty Dumpty?"

"Of course. Every kid knows that story."

"He didn't fall. He was pushed."

"Pushed? Whoever you are, you're nuts. Everyone knows he had a 'great fall'."

"Wrong."

"Okay, so, just who in the hell pushed him?"

"His ego. Just as yours is pushing you. You have allowed your ego to stand in the way of making things right with your friend. He's the one who laid down his life for you and asked nothing in return. You rejected him because he was hurt, worried, and scared. You haven't learned much, have you?"

"Esaugetuh? Where are you? Stop this damn cat and mouse business right now!"

"I am wherever you are."

"Esaugetuh!"

Silence was my answer.

It's impossible to describe the frustration these out-of-no-where visits cause. The personal turmoil because they always seem to be critical of my behavior in some way or another. I am only a man, not a perfection. At least, I think I'm still human.

To relieve my frustration I decided to walk back to the Old Town Plaza. The old saying of 'three times and you're out' could just as well be 'three times and you're in.' Maybe my third visit would be the lucky one.

The evening was pleasant as only as southwestern evening can be. In keeping with the laid back atmosphere, I slowed my pace. Others seemed to have had the same idea and just lazed along. Quite a few were strolling toward the Plaza. As I neared the Plaza, I heard the soft wail of a flute singing the Blues. That explained the number of people.

I started to cross the street just this side of the church. Stopped. Changed my mind. Memory of a past experience here came back and I was not interested in tangling with another car. I circled the park and then crossed the street, coming up behind the gazebo. Working my way around I finally found a spot and sat down on the grass.

A single figure at the center of the gazebo had that f lute talking smooth and easy. Bourbon Street would be proud of this player whoever he was. As the music moved its player, his dancing became so totally sensual that it brought the women in the audience to their feet. Mixed with heated applause were sucking sounds and whistles. Cat-like the player danced down the gazebo steps and headed through the approving crowd. I caught a glimpse of long blue-black hair falling over bare shoulders. A single red-tipped feather stuck in a white beaded headband, a loincloth, and deerskin moccasins created a picture in stark contrast to the music he played making it a statement of irony. The music stopped and so did the dancer.

"Adam."

"Running-water. Nice to see you." I said.

"Is it?"

I didn't get a change to answer because the crowd began clamoring for more and autograph seekers wanted his signature. Some of the bolder young women began to wipe his shoulders and chest with torn pieces of their own clothing and then tucking them into their bras. A few tucked them elsewhere.

"I'm at—."

"I know," Running-water said as he began to play and danced his way back into the crowd.

I left and returned to my hotel. My rib cage was killing me. I thought I would not make it to my room. Once inside I cried out,

"What is it you want of me?"

"You know what you are supposed to do. Apologize."

"Why me? What have I done that is wrong?"

"It is your job to heal others; not to throw up road blocks to their healing. You have a responsibility to heal both physically and spiritually. That's unfinished business!"

"Tell me what I'm apologizing for? For saving his life?"

"As I said, you are a dumb ass. Did he leave you? No, he did not. You left him and right when he was most vulnerable."

"And what if I refuse to apologize?" I said

"You don't want to go there, believe me."

A faint knock on my door ended my conversation. Then I heard a key being tried. I reached for my 9mm and put it at ready. The door swung open.

"Adam."

"You could have gotten your head blown off. How'd you get a key to my room? I thought I had better security than that."

"My uncle owns this hotel. I used to work here as a bellhop. I know where they keep the master key. Are you alone? I thought I heard you talking to someone."

"My usual conversation with the voice. So, what gives?"

"I came to apologize. I—."

"Uh uh! I'm the one who needs to apologize and I do. I—."

"Enough said, my brother," Running-water said as he grabbed and hugged me.

"Not quite. I need to settle a personal issue with you. What is the symbol of your spirit guide?"

"The cougar. Why?"

"While you were in the hospital I had given you another healing treatment and things were looking very grim I saw a cougar's shadow on the wall. It turned and looked at me. It was then I saw your soul. I put my arms around it, held it for just an instant, and then brought it back to you. After that, the cougar moved on. Marrie is totally wrong. I am not the one who snatches souls. You are not an IT; you will not live alone.

"There is nothing, you understand, absolutely nothing to prevent you from fathering as many kids as any wife will allow! Esaugetuh told me you were my soul-mate, that you were my protector, and that our Spirits were unalterably entwined. As I live so shall you.

"For some reason, I could not combat the emotionality of the situation at Jedediah's. And there is one other thing you must understand. You may not wish to continue paying the price to be my protector. I will not ask you to do so, nor will I resent you if you decide to follow another path. It's your choice."

"Isn't my choice obvious? I am here. You've had your say now it's my turn. I want to talk about this 'soul-mate' business. I thought soul-mates were male and female so how can we be soul-mates?"

"You're not alone. That was my understanding in the beginning. Actually, a soul-mate may be anyone, even a sibling. Sex has nothing to do with it. A soul-mate is one who shares in the development of another, spiritually and personally."

"What you're saying is that any two people regardless of their sex and biological relationship can be soul-mates?"

"Yes, but it's a unique and special relationship. Soul-mates share the same 'brain pants' and are not duplicated anywhere else in the universe. They are eternal and are drawn together because they share the same spiritual center," I said.

"Suppose I buy into this soul-mate business can you still explain what transpired between us?"

"The harmony that we shared was destroyed. We allowed its destruction by mistrust, suspicion, and fear. It drove us into the darkness of alienation. It is now necessary for each of us to change the negative patterns that have developed, the baseness of our beings."

"What do you mean by the baseness of our beings?"

"Our individual egos. They denied our individual Soul-Selves, the *I-of- the I-am.*"

"What has to be done to do to bring back the relationship we once had?" Running-water said.

"Nothing. It's done."

"Okay. By the way, I deposited the check from your father's life insurance into your account along with the balance of the cash you put in my backpack. I did keep some cash out to get me out here."

"What's with Jedediah? He was different when I called to tell him your mother was on her way out to meet Marrie and him?"

"Marrie was pissed because I wanted to find you. She says you carry death with you wherever you go. She's not a grateful woman, Adam. Her attitude is that she is owed. I think Jedediah longs for his former lifestyle and he probably blames you for interfering," Running-water said.

"I understand. It has concerned me that I may have gone overboard in doing for them. I thought perhaps Jedediah resented his home being modernized."

"No, I think he's really grateful for that. He may send Marrie packing. She is so bitter. Don't we have a couple more names left on the list?" Running-water said.

"Indeed we do, but first I want you to tell me about what you experienced at the hospital in Williamsport. Did you know that your soul had left your body? What did it feel like? Did you travel and if so where? What was it like?"

"Man you sure are full of questions. I don't know if I can explain it. I have struggled with that whole scenario for weeks. Even know I wake up in the night in a cold sweat."

"Try. It's important." I said.

CHAPTER 13 - THE OTHER SIDE

Blessedly ripe are those who radiate from a new self within; they shall be shown a waking vision.
Matthew 5:7 (from the Aramaic)

Running-water stretched out full length on the bed, folded his arms across his broad chest, and closed his eyes. Taking a blanket from the other bed, I covered him.

"What's that for? I'm not going to sleep."

"I sensed a lowering of your body temperature and with nothing on but that loincloth I was concerned. I'm not sure how well you are right now. "

"Aren't we being the old mother hen," Running-water said.

"You worked up quite a sweat with the flute and dance at the Plaza. By the way, are you wearing anything under that loincloth? The women were sure getting their panties in a sweat."

"You want to see?" Running-water said as he flipped up his loincloth to reveal a pair of briefs with red hearts.

We both laughed. And it was good to laugh again.

"I am a lawyer you know. You think I wanted to get busted for indecent exposure?"

"Maybe it would be better if we waited a few weeks more before you attempt to relive your experience on the other side. I'm not getting a really strong sense of well-being from you," I said.

"Look, didn't you say it was important to you?"

"Yes, but it is not worth a drain on your health."

"Cut the crap. It's no big thing. So I'm a little tired. I just did a two hour nonstop show."

"Okay, if you're sure. Relax as much as possible and then slowly try to go back to when you collapsed in the motor home. Begin there with your memories. What feelings is that experience generating?" I said.

"This is not going to work. I feel dumb laying here and you playing Freud. Let's sit at the table, have a drink, and just talk."

"Okay, I'll order some coffee or soda."

"No soda. I meant a shot of that aged brandy you got stashed away."

"Ah, that's in the motor home. I'll order from the bar if you like?"

"I like," Running-water said as he eased himself into a chair at the table in front of the window.

From there one could almost see to the Plaza. Street light haloes played off the nearby buildings. In the distance, the beautiful mountains created a mystical and shadowy world as moonlight filtered down to create a postcard view. Albuquerque may not be one of *the* beautiful night cities of the world like New York or Paris but its cadence is nothing short of exquisite. A quiet knock on our door broke the moment. Our drinks had arrived.

"I remember feeling very tired so very tired," Running-water began. "I just wanted to sleep. I felt warm and safe and then suddenly I felt a chilly breeze sweep over my body and I knew— I knew that I was dying. Adam close your eyes for a moment. What do you see?" Running-water said.

"Nothing."

"That's death. Nothing! Nada! Yet in a strange way, you are aware of that nothingness. Most people would say that if you are aware you are alive. You are and you aren't. There was no pain, only a weakness. I felt weightless, that is bodiless, and at the same time, I felt there was something material about my being. It seemed to me that I was floating in space, farther, and farther away from where my body actually lay.

"Other beings were present, translucent beings that seemed to be directing me. We came to a mysterious place and when I looked into its blackness, I was looking down at the earth. There was a spiraling rainbow creating a bridge from earth to where I was and along this multi-colored pigmentations were ethereal creatures dressed in flowing colorless gowns. Even though I knew they were looking at me, I could detect no eyes.

"As I continued to survey my surroundings, fiery creatures were going and coming and they had human beings between them who seemed to be screaming yet I heard no sounds. My hosts moved me to another level and from there I could see six wonderful golden columns of light traveling right up through the heavens, circling, and coming back through the earth, forming a marvelous vibrating belt. Suddenly these six columns were joined by a seventh, huge and overpowering in its light. I was sure God himself had come but then a strange thing happened."

"And that was," I said, fascinated by the story.

"I felt something tighten around me like a girdle, strong, and unyielding. A warmth flowed over me, growing ever warmer as the tightness increased, but not hurtful. It was more of a secure feeling. Then I heard a voice," Running-water said, taking a sip of his brandy.

"Do you recall what that voice said?"

"It cried out, *No*. It was more of a command. ' *No, not now!*'"

"Then what?"

"I felt something hot and wet fall onto my face. I opened my eyes and saw you standing by my bed, holding my hand, and crying. I thought I was dead but

Marrie yelled out at that moment and I knew I was alive."

"So, there was a battle for your soul!"

"What does that mean?" Running-water said.

"Two things. We had a melding of our souls and fought off those who would take yours away, and second, it confirms that we are indeed soul-mates."

"Is it true you offered one of your kidneys for me?" Running-water said.

"Yes, it was no big deal."

"It's sure been an interesting trade off," Running-water said.

"Trade off?"

"Yeah. I prevented you from getting knocked off and you gave me my life back. I think I got the better part of the deal."

After that, we sat in silence and continued to sip the brandy.

"Adam," Running-water said, "There's a couple of other things I'd like to talk about if you are open to further talk."

"Shoot. What's on your mind?"

"I'd like to talk about the human soul. Will you talk to me about that?"

CHAPTER 14 - SOUL TALK

**And the Lord God formed man of the dust of the ground, and
breathed into his nostrils the breath of life, and man became a living soul.**

Genesis 2:7

At some point in every person's life, they stop and wonder about their interior design. Not the physical-biological stuff but what it is that designates them as different from other things. Not the typical identifiers of thumb, walking erect, or speech. Certainly not the old cliché of *intelligence.* Other creatures have demonstrated considerable intelligence, even mirror recognition. And there is, of course, that wonderful identifier of emotions. How many times have you heard that only man can feel? How can one say that a dog or cat has no feelings? Or a deer, bear, eagle, or cougar? Do we really know?

I remember a question from a 'life-science' class when I was in sixth grade. The teacher told us to look at a canary he had in a cage and then asked if we thought it was aware of its existence. The eager ones in the class all said yes. Then the teacher asked, "Do you think it has a purpose other than to breed and hatch babies, come spring?" One girl said its purpose was to sing and to add joy in the world. Another classmate said the bird's purpose was to eat insects and keep them from biting us. Still, another said the bird's purpose was to provide feathers for making things. Then the teacher called on me. I remember it because I never got a reply to my answer to the question. Anyway, the teacher asked me if I thought the bird was aware of its existence.

I said, "If I pulled out one of its feathers wouldn't it feel pain? And wouldn't that tell me it was aware of its existence?"

Before the teacher could respond, another student asked the teacher if the bird had a soul. His immediate reply was "Of course not. What a stupid question." and it was said with such disdain that I wondered why. Maybe he wanted us to know that science people didn't believe in such things as souls. Whatever it was, he didn't bother to respond to my question. It was such a put down. I don't want Running-water to feel his questions are stupid or that he doesn't deserve honest answers.

If I learned anything from Esaugetuh, it was to respect the question and then to check to see if it was the right question, to see if the question could be rephrased in a way to make its intent clearer. I have since wondered what it was about the soul that my sixth grade science teacher didn't like. Running-water had asked if we could talk about the soul. I figured he really wanted to talk about his soul!

"What about the soul, Running-water?" I said.

"Well, as a Native American with a different tradition, I was taught not about a soul but about Spirit and that not only do humans have Spirits but so do all things. However, because of my mother's concern for Daphne and my welfare, she also insisted that we attend a parochial school and it was there that I learned of the soul. She even had us baptized as well as giving us Christian names. Unfortunately, I still don't know what a soul is. You said you fought a battle for my soul but did not mention my spirit. What do you mean by soul? Did you lose my spirit?"

Along with the question, "Is there a God?" his question presents the most perplexing of religious-philosophical issues. Just because I have or am going through some kind of transformation doesn't necessarily mean I have the answers. Yet, if I am to render respect to my friend and his questions, I must give him some form of an answer. Like a sound that finally penetrates one's consciousness, I became aware of his intense staring at me.

"Volumes have been written about the soul and now much is being written about spirit. An analogy might be helpful. The soul is to man what an acorn is to the great oak, the ground of being. It is his bridge to all that is divine in the universe. As I understand it, even in your traditions, there is a link to that which is sacred."

"Acorn, bridge, link do not tell me what the soul is. Those words suggest function. You wrapped your arms around my soul, forced it back to my body and you can't tell me what it is, what it looked like? How can that be?" Running-water said.

"I have to agree with you about function. Running-water, I'm not sure I can tell you about your soul. You told me you felt my tears on your face. They were not tears of sorrow. No, my brother, they were tears of overwhelming joy caused by being in the presence of absolute beauty. If each person really reflected his or her soul, the world would be more brilliant than the sun itself. Your soul was like the colors reflected in mother of pearl, moving, flowing together in an endless luminance."

"Did it look like me? How did you know it was my soul? What shape was it?"

"Whew! You're getting as bad as I am with the endless questions. Your soul did not physically look like you. It had no specific shape. It was ever moving; flowing in and out, folding and unfolding, creating a vibration I could feel. Perhaps sense is better than feel." I said.

"But how did you know that particular thing was my soul?"

"I saw it leave your body and that's when I yelled, 'No! Not now!'."

"But couldn't that have been an illusion, a ruse to keep you occupied while the 'spirit/soul snatcher did her work?"

"Ah! So that is your concern. I can dispel that once and for all."

"How?" Running-water said.

"Each of us has identifying characteristics that tell others who we are. Additionally, each of us possesses an essence that is uniquely our own and I'm not talking DNA here. I'm talking about something far more important. I am talking about the very thing that constitutes our humanness. Because you and I are soul-mates, there was a total and complete bonding when I wrapped my arms around you. Had it not been your soul there is a very strong likelihood that both of us would be dead."

"You're absolutely sure?"

"Yes! Absolutely sure! However, I sense there is more to your concern. What's really bothering you?"

"Dreams. Strange ugly dreams. They were so bad at Jedediah's that I would wake them up with my screaming. It got to the point that I couldn't stand it any longer so I packed up and came back here hoping that being in my own territory would make them go away. It's a funny thing Adam, but I knew you would be here."

"Speaking of being back, did you call your mother or uncle?"

"No. I'm not ready for their questions. Don't you think you should have heard from Dutch by now? Seems to me they should have landed."

On cue, the cell phone vibrated. It was Dutch. He wanted to know what to do. Marrie Copa apparently has lost it, Jedediah wants to come west, and Cornelia wants to return. According to Dutch, Marrie has become violent, spending her time conjuring and trying to cast spells or something to that effect. Jedediah is also certain that she is not his long lost childhood sweetheart. He has had her put in a local nursing home.

For some time, I had felt that Marrie Copa was more than an old lady. I believe she is the real 'spirit/soul' snatcher. I was battling her for Running-water. Several things have led me to those feelings.

When she first met Running-water at her apartment, she gave no indication that she recognized any family resemblance. When Running-water told me, she knew about the dead men outside of her apartment she began talking in her own language and it wasn't to the men in the next room. She was uttering a curse.

Certainly, the sudden arrival of dozens of people outside of the hospital should have made me wonder. It was obvious they came to protect. I also thought it strange that she made such a big issue of Running-water's future, telling him his life would be one of loneliness, of being childless, and of being asexual. There were other things, little things just on the edge of being realized but never quite focused; the massage with the ointment that caused the chief of staff at the hospital to say there was the smell of death about Running-water and her insistence of using her herbal tea. I now wonder if she really is Marrie Copa and if she's not, who is she?

"Running-water, can you do a background check on Marrie?"

" What do you want to know?"

"As much as you can find out. In the meantime, I'll call Sheriff Logan and ask him to get a set of fingerprints, and a blood sample from the nursing home. I think Marrie Copa tried to kill you and I think she killed the two men outside of her apartment. For all, I know she may have killed Esaugetuh."

"Damn. Maybe it wasn't Randolph, maybe it's been Marrie all along. Okay, let me get my lap top. You want me to move in with you. If what you think is true, mutual back-up might be a good idea."

"Wouldn't have it any other way. Let's stop at the front desk and see if we can get a suite with limited access. It might be a good idea not to tell Jedediah you are in the hotel."

"What's the story on Jedediah? You know something I don't?"

"He may be under Marrie's influence. I don't know of any reason for his sudden desire to come here. He may be her unknowing henchman. Caution is the rule from now on."

"You really think he may try to knock you off?"

"You may be the target. Take no unnecessary chances. I didn't tell Dutch you were here, however; Jedediah may have told your mother that you are back in Albuquerque. I don't recommend that you meet the plane. I'll tell him you have an apartment but not tell him where it's located."

"Okay, just don't let my mother know about the apartment. Since my aunt's death, my uncle comes into the city at least once a month, picks up a lady for the weekend. It's our little secret. I get the apartment the rest of the time if I want it.

"Come on. You've got to be kidding. Your mother knows you get laid," I said.

"It's not me. It's my uncle, her brother. She'd think he was being disrespectful to his deceased wife.

"I'll notify Dutch that there will be a car to take her home and that Jedediah is to be brought here. I think he and Brett now need to be on the alert as well. Marrie's so called breakdown may be a ruse. If she is really trying to conjure up shamanistic powers, she's probably in a trance in an effort to communicate with the Other Side. If she was to deliver up your soul and failed, she's in trouble and may be trying to redeem herself. If this turns out to be true, she is far more dangerous than anything we've faced. We'll need every advantage we can muster. Let's get that lap top," I said.

We stopped by Running-water's room, picked up the lap top, and took the elevator to the main floor. While he was connecting to the Internet, I asked about a suite. There were two available on the top floor. I took both of them. This would help assure our safety since access to the top floor was by keyed elevator only. I also asked about stairways and the roof top. That done, I joined Running-water in the ante room they had set up for computer users.

"Running-water did you ever see Marrie without her shoes on?" I said.

"Sure. After dinner, she would sit in the rocking chair, kick her shoes off, and go to sleep. Why?"

"What did her feet look like?" I said.

"Normal feet for an old woman. What's so important about her feet?"

"The Marrie I met had very crippled feet; her toes were all curved under. I had asked the doctor to see about doing something about them and to contact me. He never did. That woman, whoever she is, is not Marrie Copa."

"There's another thing," Running-water said. "Those two creeps who tried to knock us off in the desert knew where to find us. We assumed Randolph had sent them but Marrie was the only one who knew where we were going. This woman who claims to be Marrie could have sent them. And if she did, where is the real Marrie Copa?"

"Hmm. You could be right. Once you're finished with the computer search let's see if we can get in touch with the hospital back in Arizona," I said as I turned to go back to the main lobby.

I didn't tell Running-water everything I had noticed about his soul. It would have upset him further. His soul was in considerable disharmony. Because of the trauma, he had experienced this was to be expected. Beyond that, I noted a sense of loss, a profound and specific sorrow whose cause I could not detect. Whatever the cause, the sorrow ran deep— a dark shadow that draped itself around the center of his being. This woman who has passed herself off as Marrie Copa may very well have tuned into this sorrow and used it against him. She might still try to do that. An uneasiness that had been lurking beneath the surface of my conscious expressed itself. My body gave an involuntary shudder.

The pressure of my 'manifest destiny' gnawed at my guts. Resentment over Esaugetuh's disappearance steadily grew and uncertainty about my own abilities seemed to increase minute by minute. I am a white man with a gift to heal. My knowledge of the shamanistic powers held by Esaugetuh is not totally mine to call upon. What's more, they never may be. Some Native Americans have thought I was the "lost white brother." I don't believe I am. True, Esaugetuh adopted me and had begun his instruction but never completed it. It is also true that he has spoken to me from another dimension but now I even question that. Hell, those *conversations* with him could have been just my imagination or my subconscious creating other worlds not dissimilar to what occurs during lucid dreaming. One thing was certain; people have tried to kill Running-water and me. It now appears that there have been at least two distinct groups who have wanted us out of the way. The Randolph issue is over and settled. That leaves Marrie.

I watched Running-water come out of the ante room and into the lobby. His cock-sure attitude told me he had found something important.

"Guess what?" Running-water said,

"What?"

"Marrie Copa has a twin and she is alive. Lives near Durango."

"Does your uncle know a good private detective?"

"I'm sure he's used one at some time or another. I usually did his leg work for him. Why?"

"I want to have him track down Marrie Copa's sister."

"What's wrong with my doing it?"

"I would like you to check on something else."

My cell phone vibrated. It was Dutch. They had just landed. I told him to be on his guard.

"Running-water let's go to your mother's. I'd like to ask her a few questions about the people who raised your father. Brett will take care of Jedediah."

"I don't know. She's never really talked about my father or indicated anything about any grandparents. She might have some memories tucked away."

It took us about thirty minutes. We arrived just as Dutch was pulling into Cornelia's driveway.

The warm yet reserved greeting she gave her only son surprised me, especially after the firry reception, I was given. It was the kind of greeting one used for public appearances. Once inside the house, it was a different story. She let him have it. She really chewed out his ass, big time. And just as suddenly, she realized she had two other people in her house. Her face flushed.

"Adam wants to ask you some questions about my father," Running-water said.

"About your father?"

"Well, actually about the people who raised him," I said.

"Let me put on some tea and while I'm doing that Paul, you can get out the family photos."

Another surprise in the mother son relationship. She used his Christian name.

She brought us tea and I knew that Dutch really wanted a beer but he showed some grace and accepted it anyway. As I reached to accept my cup from Cornelia, she screamed and dropped the cup, spilling the hot tea on my hand and forearm. She stood frozen with her hand at her open mouth.

"Don't just stand there mother. For God's sake. Do something. You've scalded Adam's arm," Running-water said grabbing my arm, patting it dry with a napkin.

"Don't make such a fuss. It really didn't burn me," I protested.

"Holy shit!"

"What?" I said.

"How long has that sign been on your wrist?" Running-water said.

"It's just a small scar. Probably got it at my parents' house when I was

moving stuff in the basement."

"Really look at it, Adam. Take a real close look."

"It's just a line with some jagged edges," I said.

"No! It's an eagle's feather and a bolt of lightning above it. It's a sign of great power. Only the most powerful of shamans are marked that way. You are marked! Esaugetuh has transferred his powers."

"Let me put some cream on that hand," Cornelia said. "Oh! It's not even red."

"The cut on my wrist frightened you. Why?"

"I've seen pictures of it and heard stories of those who had it. I take pride in being an educated person but I have to admit there are some things that are beyond normal understanding. There are those who are above what we perceive as normal. Most are to be feared," Cornelia said.

"That's what Marrie wanted to prevent, you from coming to full power. She'll come after you with hell's fury. Under no circumstance am I going to let you out of my sight. Dutch get in touch with Brett and tell him to be ready for the battle of his life," Running-water said.

"Just hold on," I said. "You are going to Lake Tahoe. Furthermore, I want your mother and your uncle out of the state. We need to deal with Jedediah and then I'll deal with Marrie, whoever she is. Where is your sister, Daphne? Make sure she stays away. I want you to understand that it is absolutely necessary for you to do as I say. No arguments, no change in plans."

"What's with this Tahoe shit?" Running-water said.

"Tell you on our way to the hotel. Cornelia, call your brother and have him meet you at the airport. The two of you are taking an island vacation. Dutch once you have them on the island, return here. Meet us at the hotel. I'll send Brett back to the airport. Come on, Running-water we've work to do."

While Running-water drove, I sat in silence. The gun strapped under my arm didn't make me feel any better. The violence has sickened me. Perhaps this thing with Marrie's twin will end it once and for all. Surely, Esaugetuh must be ashamed of me because of all the deaths I've caused. There's one thing I must do and that's to insure Running-water's safety. And the best place for that is among the Cathedral of Trees seated within the circle of seven stones. It is sacrosanct and beyond her reach.

"Before you leave for Tahoe you must cleanse yourself, go into a fast, and prepare yourself for extended prayer. You must be able to give yourself over to the sanctity of the place in the deep woods. It is important that you remain there until I come for you in your dreamtime. Here, you will need this to light the fire in the sacred circle of stones. The fire will help you enter the dreamtime," I said handing him a small pinch from Esaugetuh's medicine. "You must do this for me."

"How is that going to help you fight the evil one? I don't get it."

"I have no family she can hold captive You will be out of her range of power and she can't use you against me. With your family removed from her geography, they also will be safe."

"What about Jedediah? What are we going to do about him?"

"We will both greet him at the hotel. If he doesn't attempt to hug you first I'll know he is under the influence of Marrie's twin sister."

" So what happens if he greets you first?"

"He will die!"

"Is that necessary? I mean, why does he have to die? He's my grandfather. His blood runs through me."

"His soul may have been taken from him. If so, he is no longer your grandparent. In some parts of the world, people would call him a zombie. Don't even consider stepping between us if he should come to me first."

We continued the ride to the hotel in silence. As we approached the hotel, I saw Jedediah walking along the street. It seemed to me that he was walking straighter than when I last saw him. His gait wasn't any faster nor was it any slower. There was no shuffling of his feet. That was a good sign. However, he turned and looked directly at me and even through the tinted car window, I could see his eyes had changed. That was not good.

"Damn!" I said.

"What"? Running-water said.

"It's Jedediah. He's spotted me. Stop the car and let me out."

As I got out of the car, Jedediah came to greet me. He opened his arms to hug me. Just as he was about to wrap his arms around me a voice from above the hotel facade yelled, "Look out below. Hot wire!"

The wire, flaying back and forth like a wounded snake seemed to be searching for me. Jedediah stepped back, turned toward the wire and as he did, it reached up and clipped him beside the head. He collapsed, thrashed for a moment, and then lay still. A ground crewman caught the wire with a hook and dragged it back toward the hotel wall. Jedediah was dead. We'll never know what would have happened had he hugged me. All I know is that he saved my life. Running-water knelt beside his grandfather, placed a finger on each eye lid, and closed them. He said nothing, got up, and went into the hotel. A crowd had gathered and a frantic hotel manager was yelling on a cell phone. An ambulance arrived and removed the body.

Inside the hotel, another problem greeted me. The clerk had allowed two men into our suite.

"Why did you allow these men into my suite when I gave specific orders that no one was to be allowed on that floor?

"They said they were from the FBI. I had to let them go up."

"Did they have a warrant?" Running-water said.

"I don't know. What difference does it make? They are FBI."

"All the difference in the world. Call hotel security and the local police. I want them out of my suite immediately and I want them arrested," I said.

"Do it now!" Running-water growled.

The hotel security got the two and brought them to the main lobby. The local police had arrived. I recognized the two men from Marrie Copa's apartment, the same two who gave us their jeep and brought us ammunition to the plane.

"Why are you here and how did you know where we were?" I said.

"Marrie Copa's disappeared. We came to get your help in finding her. We knew you were here because we got your flight plan. We called the hotels and found you were registered here," said the larger of the two men.

"Why the FBI ruse?" Running-water said.

"We called the hotel and was told you were registered but wasn't in. When we got here, they told us no one by the name of Adam was registered. Figured you were here and we wanted to make sure we saw you," said the larger man.

"You have a name?" I said.

"Joseph."

"Well, Joseph, why was it so important for you to go to my rooms rather than wait for me here in the lobby?"

"Didn't want anyone to know we had come. Didn't want anyone to see us talking to you. Did not want Paú guk to know where you were."

"Paú guk?" I said.

"It means Flying Skelton Death Spirit," Joseph said.

"You still have not said why you are here?" Running-water said.

"Something's happened to Marrie."

"What do you mean?" I said.

"We had come to her place to talk to you because she wanted you to go into the desert for healing. While we were waiting for you to come back from Flagstaff, a woman came to her door. Don't know what she said. Whatever it was,

Marrie took a real fright. She went to a chair, sat down, and just stared straight ahead."

"And," I said.

" We left and came back later. She was very uneasy. Didn't have much to say. We tried to talk to her about you going off into the desert and perhaps she should have gone with you. She didn't want to talk," Joseph said.

"Why didn't you tell me this at the airport at Flagstaff?" I said.

"We tried but you were in a big hurry," Joseph said.

I remembered and regretted my haste and rudeness. Next time I would listen.

"Did you notify the police that she was missing?" Running-water said.

"Yes. They found nothing," Joseph said.

"Nothing?" Running-water said.

"No trace of her anywhere?" I said.

"Nothing. Everything in her apartment was as it always was. It's like

Marrie has disappeared from the face of the earth." Joseph said.

"We'll find her. Don't worry," I said.

"You'll have to excuse us we have an appointment. Do you have a place

to stay?" I said.

"Don't worry about us. We have relatives."

CHAPTER 15 - BEGINNING OR END

**Only in absolute stillness, beyond self, can you know Me as I am,
and then but as a feeling and a faith.
James Dillet Freeman**

The information Running-water turned up indicated that Marrie Copa had a twin sister, Isabella Watrus, or Moon Woman. Because of Running-water's knowledge of information data sources, he was able to get an address and a social security number.

An e-mail to Daphne, his twin sister, brought some additional information. Isabella lived in a small border town, never married, and was a practitioner of the dark arts. A phone call to her residence got a recording. As soon as I was sure, Running-water was on his way to Tahoe I set out for Moon Woman's home. I also contacted Dutch who was already airborne to tell him where I was going.

At this point, I didn't know if Isabella knew where Cornelia or her brother lived. It wasn't clear how she connected with Marrie and why she had decided to go after Running-water. Despite the terrible sense of danger that engulfed me, I felt calm and energized. Maybe that was because I also felt Esaugetuh's presence.

At Saint-Michaels' island retreat, he told me he was always with me. Even during my experience in the parallel universe, he was there. His strength and love, cocoon-like, wrapped around me, a protective shield. Instinctively I knew that I needed help with Moon Woman. However, as soon as that thought materialized a dread, sickening and terrible replaced it.

Is it because I am afraid to die? No, it wasn't a sense of death that terrorized me. He had been met and rebuffed long ago. Is it the possible loss of Runningwater, my protector, and friend? No, we have crossed that bridge already and know that our united souls are eternal. Why then do I have this overriding sense of dread? Change perspective and perception will change is what Esaugetuh always told me to do.

Okay, so how do I deal with Moon Woman? I don't know! Not knowing has always been the bane of my life. Not knowing has cast doubt upon my very existence. Doubt is my saboteur, self-doubt, unbridled, destroys potentiality before it has a change to begin.

It seems to me that the best way to deal with Moon Woman's all-consuming hatred is not to reflect it back. My tone, actions, even my eyes must not reflect hate. To prepare myself for my encounter with Moon Woman, I felt it necessary to bring my spirituality back into harmony. Before entering the small town where she lived, I decided to purify myself. I left the main road and headed into the desert, stopped near an outcropping of red rocks, a good place for a purification ceremony.

I laid out seven round stones in a circle, each seven inches apart just as Esaugetuh had taught me. In the center, I built a small teepee of sweet grass and from it, I laid out seven pieces of sage that formed the spokes of my sacred wheel. Next, I removed all of my clothes taking care to pile them a safe distance from the wheel. Then I took a pinch of power from my medicine pouch and sprinkled it over the seven stalks of sage.

Sitting cross-legged I watched the sage begin to smolder and I smudged it over my body; first to my abdomen, next to my chest and then to my head. Small flames began to lick at the base of my sweet grass teepee and it burst into flames.

The perfumed smoke surrounded me and I began to pray to all the present and past Spirits, to my father, the sky and to my mother, the earth. I asked them to give me strength but above all to grant me wisdom as I prepared to meet this latest challenge. I remained at prayer until I began to feel the coolness of the desert caress my nakedness. Refreshed and spiritually secure, I quickly dressed, got into the car, and headed for Moon Woman's house.

The house, actually a dilapidated shack made of tar paper and pieces of aluminum, was boarded up. Two broken cinderblocks served as steps. The yard weed grown, seemed to struggle against an invasion of papers and uncollected mail that lay scattered about. Even though it was obvious that no one was there, still I knocked on the door. No answer.

I went around back. I pulled a piece of plywood from a window, pushed upward with the heel of my hand and the window opened. Once inside I fumbled around in the dark and found a light switch. It turned on a single small watt bulb hanging from the ceiling.

The smell was nauseating and the light roused hordes of sleeping flies. I unlocked the back door and pushed it open. Cautiously I moved to the next room. Death's smell was everywhere. Dozens of rattlers slithered in front of me, some coiling to strike. Evil guardians of an evil place. I raised my right hand, drew a circle in the air with it and the snakes silenced themselves and crawled back into the walls of the house. Esaugetuh always said to calm a beast use the circle

I stumbled against something. It felt soft and slippery. I found a second light switch and like the first, it turned on a single naked bulb hanging from the ceiling. My stomach did a flip flop when I saw what I had stumbled against, the remains of a human body. Decay and insects had done their job. A piece of red cloth remained across what was once its mouth and its hands and feet were tied with the same red cloth. The stench was making me nauseous. I left the house gasping for fresh air. Once I was able to stop vomiting, I called 911 and waited for the Tribal Police to arrive.

Two men, displaying the swagger typical of the young, guns hung low, and arms held at the ready, identified themselves. I told them what I found in the house. One came back out and vomited. Another police vehicle arrived and an older man, forty-something, got out of his car. He was tall, lean, and muscular. His face bore a scar about two inches in length and like Runningwater's uncle, his nose was flat because of the number of times it had been broken.

"I'm Sam Western, chief of police. Why you snoopin' around Isabella's place?"

"I'm Adam," I said extending my hand. "I'm looking for Isabella and her twin sister, Marrie Copa. Marrie's husband was killed in an accident."

He had taken notice of the shamanic icon on my wrist.

"Didn't know Moon Woman had a sister. People here 'bouts didn't much like he," Chief Western said, his tone changing.

"Not liked?" I said.

"She spooked a lot of people 'cause she was into the black arts. Some said she was a witch while others said she was the devil himself. How'd you say the sister's husband died?"

"I didn't. A high voltage wire that fell from a hotel roof top struck him."

"Fried. What a way to get it. So who you think is inside?" Chief Western said.

"I don't know. I'd like the coroner's report if that's possible. Could you ask him to pay particular attention to the victim's feet?"

"No problem but what's with the feet?"

"Marrie Copa had crippled feet, her sister didn't."

"So, you think this may not be Moon Woman?"

"There's that possibility," I said.

"What makes you think that?" Chief Western said.

"Isabella Watrus was in a nursing home in Pennsylvania. Her twin has been missing from her home in Arizona for several weeks."

"It'll be a few weeks before I get a report. Where you want yours sent?"

I gave him Gordon Alexander's address. A lawyer's address would cause fewer problems.

"How can I get in touch with you?" Chief Western said.

"I'm staying in town tonight. After that, Gordon will know where I am. And Chief, thanks."

I drove on into town, had a burger and fries, checked into a motel, and waited for a call from Running-water. His call came on schedule. He was at Tahoe and was about to start his climb to the Cathedral of Trees. Just as I hung up there was a knock at my door.

It was Chief Western. Moon Woman's house was on fire and the local firemen couldn't seem to extinguish the flames. He wanted to know if I smelled gas while I was in the house. I hadn't. Once again, she was testing me to determine my strength.

"You mind riding back out there with me? You might remember seeing gas cans or something."

I went with the Chief. The shack was a mass of flames and the more water the firemen pumped into it the fiercer the flames seemed to grow. Remembering my own advice, I did not confront the flames. Instead, I sat down, cross-legged and began to meditate, allowing my whole being to fill with thoughts of beauty and a love for all living things.

The intensity of the flames as their tongues licked dangerously close to my body. I did not more nor did I swat at the flames as one would at a pesky fly. Soon, sensing no adversary, the flames quieted and died. However, as I got up a single flame rose up from the rubble, hissing loudly, it reached out to lash me. I held out my right hand and drew a circle. It sunk back to its source and went out.

"Say now, that's quite a show you just put on. How'd you do that?" Chief Western said.

"You saw the mark on my wrist. That answers your question," I said as I got into his car.

Inwardly I felt very pleased with myself. That was the first time I had knowingly used the sign of the shaman and because I made the right choice in not being confrontational.

That was short lived because a sharp pain in my rib cage snapped me out of my smugness. My inner voice reminded me that this was just a test, not even a battle, certainly not the war. Both were yet to come! Now another death. Will it never stop? What's it all for? Why me? Anger replaced the meditative calm and the pain in my rib cage became so intense that I was sure I was having a heart attack. By the time, I got back to the motel I was wringing wet from the uncontrollable spasms of pain.

The more control I tried to exert the more severe the spasms seemed to become. Once in my room, I collapsed on the bed. To keep from crying out I stuffed part of the pillow in my mouth. At what point I fell asleep I don't remember but when I awoke, it was midday and my phone was ringing.

It was Chief Western. The local coroner was his brother and he had completed a partial autopsy, enough to tell me that I had found Marrie Copa's body in Moon Woman's house. Her feet were badly crippled. The Chief had issued an all-points bulletin for Moon Woman. I thanked the Chief and then made a call to the cousins back at my hotel in Albuquerque.

"Hul-lo." It was Joseph.

"Marrie Copa is dead," I said.

"How? When?"

"Apparently she has been dead for quite some time. Cause of death has not been determined. However, I suspect she was starved to death. I am truly sorry. If there's anything I can do?"

"Uh, no, guess not," Joseph said and hung up.

Round one. I guess it's her call. I paid my motel bill and headed

back to Albuquerque where I would wait. More importantly, it was

necessary to teach Running-water thought-communication. The cell phone was not to be trusted. Staying put would give me time to do that.

I had been sending him small short messages as we rode in the

car or on the plane. I would wait and see what his actions would be. Once we had actually thought communicated I wanted him to do a visualization—to actually see me.

All of this would be necessary for my confrontation with Moon Woman. Twice she has tested me and twice she has yielded. I don't know if her withdrawal was deliberately planned or if it was because I was able to force her to withdraw.

I called Running-water one last time. He had worked his way along the high rim around Lake Tahoe. For a time he had followed old game trails and then picked up paths made by his Brothers ages before him. He was high up and well situated in the Cathedral of Trees.

Quickly I told him to thought-communicate from now on. Using the techniques I had taught him, we practiced one more time during which I instructed him in visualization. Time was limited because he was about to begin his own spiritual cleansing and go into continuous prayer. It would be while he was in deep meditation that we would visually communicate. I knew his spiritual strength would be necessary to combat Moon Woman.

If evil can be transmitted from one person to another, from one generation to another, is it not also true of love? Deep within my soul, I

know that the way to combat Moon Woman is not to combat her but to extend to her unconditional love. Somewhere in the recesses of memory, lurked the idea that if you draw a circle of love you can draw that person in.

The issue for me is to remain controlled, deliberate, and focused. A chill ran over me and I felt myself give an involuntary shudder. Doubt is my enemy; fear is my safe harbor. I must never lose sight of my own value for it is through that recognition that I can recognize it in others. Love itself is limited when there is no love of Self.

***

In the Cathedral of Trees, Running-water busied himself doing as Adam had instructed. Following the traditions of his people, he cleansed himself, and carefully laid out his medicine circle. He walked around the circle, checking its shape.

Satisfied, he then bowed to the East. His grandfathers had taught him that the East is the time of the rising sun and brings with it, clarity of vision, and the beginning of all understanding.

"O' great Spirit of the East, grant me clear vision and understanding."

Next, he placed a copper colored stone at the eastern point of his circle. Standing fully erect with arms outstretched, Running-water offered a pipe to the Spirits of the East. He stood still, paying close attention in order to receive the subtleties of the sacred powers of the East.

Slowly turning to the south, he placed a bright yellow stone at its point and again he offered up his pipe. Sensing a good deal of activity, he allowed it to bathe him, seeking whatever strength was being offered.

Turning and bowing to the west, he placed a black stone at its point. He didn't immediately offer the pipe. It is here, he thought, that I must look into myself, for it is said that the power of evil, as well as beauty, resides there. If I am to be of any help to Adam I have to be sure that, I feel no ill will toward anyone, that I harbor no resentments. Once his mind was calm, he offered the pipe to the Spirits of the West.

To the north, he bowed and placed a white stone at its point. North was the center of wisdom and he knew that he would have to act with more than mere knowledge. If he didn't it could mean Adam's death. He offered a pipe and then placed it at his feet. He sat down and began to pray to the Spirits of place, to his ancestors, and to the Spirits of the four directions.

"Spirits of my ancestors make me worthy. Help me to honor you with courage and conviction."

The hours slipped into days and during this time, he took no food or water. Seated in his position of prayer Running-water paused in his meditation and looked at the great trees that surrounded him. He noted their strength, size, and grace.

One particularly large tree caught his attention and he followed it upward and looked into the heavens above him. Dark ominous clouds were forming. Daylight disappeared. A blue-white flash severed the dark clouds and in obedience, they parted revealing a whirling mass of unimaginable magnitude—an aerial Charybdis. [15]

The fierceness of this heavenly convolution numbed his whole being. His eyes were transfixed as two figures unfurled themselves; the massive clouds gave way to define them. Both were seated, shadowy figures, giants from another world. Great flashes of intense lightening emanated from one figure. It was so intense Running-water was sure he could smell the smoke from the tall trees that trembled above him.

Horrid hate reached down and griped his heart, squeezing it until he felt it was going to burst. He was sure he was going to die.

"You have no right to be in this sacred place," Running-water screamed.

Beads of perspiration slithered down his naked chest and ended at his root. His long blue-black hair was matted to his head. Even though his crossed legs begged for relief from inactivity, he could not turn his eyes from the scene unfurling above him. The intensity of the lightening finally lessened; he was now able to focus on the other seated figure.

Around this figure was a radiant glowing orb, a rainbow of translucent colors. It seemed to encompass the whole of the figure itself. The more the first figure unleashed bolts of lightning at the orb the larger it grew. The earth was shaking as though it was in a fit of palsy.

The hooves of frightened running animals shook the ground beneath where he sat. Even the birds took wing. Once he was sure, he heard human voices crying out, lost souls seeking salvation from whatever terrors they felt. Several large rocks came very close as they whizzed by. Yet, he remained in his position, unmoving and transfixed.

For Adam's sake, I will die here, he thought.

First, he felt it, sensed it, then he heard it. Adam, fighting for his life, was calling him. As though it had been preprogrammed, Running-water's spirit raced to join the raging battle above him.

Like Michelangelo's wondrous painting of God reaching out to Adam, Running-water saw the outstretched hand and grabbed it. At that instant, there was such a violent burst that the entire heavens were set ablaze. Where there had been darkness there was light, atomic in its very nature. The orbed figure seemed to fill the heavens and they stilled themselves, becoming calm and quiet.

Running-water strained to make sure he was seeing what he was seeing. There were two figures in the orb. Azure blue had replaced the once ominous clouds. With a blink of an eye, the two figures were gone.

His crossed legs ached, numbed from a lack of blood flow; his stomach growled for food and, his throat cried out for moisture,

Running-water determined to remain at Tahoe until he was told to leave. He wondered where Adam was.

"Maybe," he mused, "this ends it for both of us. I stay till death removes me."

"It's not your time, my friend. We still have the seventh person on our list to find. And don't forget we still haven't found Esaugetuh." It was Adam's voice.

Despite the lack of feeling in his legs, Running-water got up and began to dance. Slow at first, but gradually increased the rhythm until he was in full dance-mode.

"Yes!" he yelled.

***

FOOTNOTES

[1] Means Master of Breath in Muskhogean.
[2] On or about 12/03/00 the Lake Tahoe area experienced an earthquake.
[3] The number seven is a sacred number to the Mik'Maq Indians, a branch of the Algonquian.
[4] A short story written in the 1880's which explores part of Tolstoy's Christian ethic
[5] Rhyolite is composed of the Greek rhyax+lite meaning stream, thus streaming rock because of its beautiful flow bands. It is locally called red rock. The rock in this area is estimated to be 1.8 billion years old.
[6] Two independent teams of physicists were successful in slowing light to a dead stop, stored it, and released it in January of 2001.
[7] SETI is the Search for Extraterrestrial Intelligence operated at UC at Berkeley.
[8] A hollow chamber whose dimensions allow the resonant oscillation of electromagnetic or acoustic waves. In this situation electromagnetic waves are to be converted into ultrasound waves at a pitch low enough for the human ear to detect.
[9] Wilson, Norman W. The Shaman's Quest. Zadkiel Publishing, 2018, 178
[10] Circa 1890 by Isapwo Muksika Crowfoot, Blackfoot Chief.
[11] Watts, Alan. Does It Matter? New York: Vintage Books, 1968, p. 85.
[12] Ibid. p. 77
[13] In the Greek myth of Orpheus and Eurydice, Orpheus goes to Hades to retrieve Eurydice. Eurydice could return to the living if Orpheus didn't look back. Just as he left the dark side, he turned to see if Eurydice was behind him. She was not allowed to continue and had to remain in Hades.
[14] A whorl is a round shape formed by a series of concentric circles. Imagine a large ice cream cone with smaller cones inside and that it is spinning like a top.
[15] Charybdis in Greek Mythology is a huge whirlpool lying on the other side of a narrow strait on whose opposite side existed Scylla, a sea monster that destroyed shipwrecked sailors.

www.ingramcontent.com/pod-product-compliance
Lightning Source LLC
Chambersburg PA
CBHW071305110426
42743CB00042B/1184